1001

words

your child will read

by the end of

Grade 1

by Nancy Laney Skultety, M.A.
Reading Specialist
Homer-Center School District
Homer City, Pennsylvania

BARRON'S

Special thanks to Beverly and Michael Mastalski, Terri Koenigsberg, Karen Sanguini, Pam Fetterman, Lisa Altemus, Angela Long, and Bev Kundla.

All inquiries should be addressed to:
Barron's Educational Series, Inc.
250 Wireless Boulevard
Hauppauge, New York 11788
http: //www.barronseduc.com

ISBN-13: 978-0-7641-3305-3 (book)
ISBN-10: 0-7641-3305-5 (book)

ISBN-13: 978-0-7641-8275-4 (CD-ROM)
ISBN-10: 0-7641-8275-7 (CD-ROM)

ISBN-13: 978-0-7641-7883-2 (package)
ISBN-10: 0-7641-7883-0 (package)

Printed in China

9 8 7 6 5 4 3 2 1

Table of Contents

This section reviews basic phonetic rules, et cetera, which are learned in first grade. The main body of the text in this book uses decodable words to help teach the 101 non-decodable words. It is important for children to grasp the idea that most words can be sounded out, while others must be memorized

per Word Group: activities include Code, Trace/Build/Write, Hidden Pictures, Grid, Maze, Circle the Picture, Word Search, Crossword Puzzle, Story Reading, and Sequencing and ABC Order

including mazes, puzzles, matching, writing, drawing, tracing and coloring exercises, fill in the blank, and short stories and poems

Cumulative Word List

about	give	says
again	good	school
all	great	shoes
always	guess	some
animal	have	soon
answer	house	story
any	how	talk
are	kind	the
around	know	their
as	laugh	there
away	lion	they
ball	look	to
because	lose	too
book	love	took
both	many	through
brother	money	very
buy	mother	walk
by	move	want
circle	my	was
climb	new	watch
color	now	water
come	of	were
could	oh	what
do	old	where
does	once	who
down	one	won
draw	only	would
every	our	write
eye	out	you
family	picture	your
father	poor	zoo
find	pretty	
food	put	
friend	said	
full	saw	

Dear Special Folks at Home:

This book contains a list of 101 non-decodable words. Non-decodable words are words that cannot be sounded out because they do not follow basic phonetic rules. These are words that need to be drilled because, to be mastered, they must simply be memorized.

Grade 1 is a critical year. The 101 words targeted in this book were selected because they are key words in developing reading fluency. The goal of this book is to provide your child with experiences with these words, so that they will know them by the end of first grade. Mastery of these words is crucial to your child's success as a reader.

This learning tool provides puzzles, matching exercises, short stories, and other activities aimed at providing your child with opportunities to use the words in sentence context and in isolation. The book was constructed this way so that once children complete the first practice set, they will be familiar with what is expected, and thus can work more independently. I hope you recognize the value in a book constructed with you and your child in mind.

This book also contains a section on decoding tips. The purpose of this section is to help you reinforce basic reading concepts taught in school.

Sincerely,

Nancy Laney Skultety

Nancy Laney Skultety

How many letters are in the alphabet? The alphabet is made up of twenty-six letters.
a b c d e f g h i j k l m n o p q r s t u v w x y z

The alphabet can be divided into two groups.
Vowels (a, e, i, o, u) and sometimes y
Consonants (b, c, d, f, g, h, j, k, l, m, n, p, q, r, s, t, v, w, x, y, z)

(Y) can be a vowel only when it is in the middle or end of a word.
y = i (example — my)
y = e (example — baby)
ay = a (example — play)

Why does the (y) in my sound like (i), like (e) in baby, and like (a) in play?
(y) will sound like (i) when it is at the end of a word that has no other vowels.
(y) will sound like (e) when it is at the end of a word that has another vowel or vowels in it.
(y) will help make the (long a sound) when it is with the letter (a).

How are vowels different from consonants?
Vowels make at least two sounds (long and short).
Consonants usually make just one sound; exceptions are (c), (g), and (x).
c = c like in cat
c = c like in circle
g = g like in go
g = g like in giraffe
x = x like in x-ray
x = ks like in six

Vowels make at least two sounds, so how do you know which sound to use?

The key is to look at the number of vowels.

Short-Vowel Rule: when a word has only one vowel, it is usually short. Examples are <u>hop</u>, <u>mad</u>, <u>pet</u>, <u>hid</u>, and <u>gum</u>.

Long-Vowel Rule: When there are two or more vowels in a one-part word or syllable, the vowel is usually long; for example, <u>road</u>, <u>please</u>, <u>gave</u>, and <u>like</u>.

Let's take a closer look. Look at the word <u>road</u>. It has two vowels. The first vowel in the word is (o). The first vowel is the vowel that determines the sound. When a word has two vowels, the sound will be the first letter's name. The second vowel doesn't make any sound, but it has a really important job, because even though it makes no sound, it is a sign for your brain to say the long sound for the first vowel.

When you are figuring out a word, look at the vowels. Think if there is one vowel or more than one. If there is only one vowel, use the short sound for the vowel in the word. If there are two or more vowels, say the long vowel sound for the first vowel.

Here are some examples.

mad — You see one vowel; therefore the (a) is short.

made — You see two vowels; therefore the (a) is long. The letter (e) was a sign for your brain to say the (long a) sound.

However, when there is only one vowel in a word and it comes at the end of the word, it is usually long. Examples are <u>go</u>, <u>me</u>, <u>so</u>, and <u>we</u>.

Note: The long- and short-vowel rules are general guidelines; some words do not follow these basic rules.

The short-vowel rule says that when there is only one vowel, the word should have a short sound, so why doesn't car have the (short a) sound?

It is because it is an r-controlled vowel word.

Usually, if a vowel is followed by an (r), the (r) will control the vowel and make it take on a whole new sound.

R-controlled vowels do not allow the vowel to say its long or short sound. Examples: <u>park</u>, <u>her</u>, <u>girl</u>, <u>hurt</u>, <u>fort</u>

When (ar) is together, the (ar) makes the sound (r). The letters (er), (ir), and (ur) all say the same sound, but spell it differently. Sometimes (or) can also say the same sound that (er), (ir), and (ur) say. However, the main sound for (or) is or like in fork.

Memory aid for er, ir, ur, and sometimes the (or) sound. Think of a rooster on a fence. He can wake up the animals in the barnyard by crowing er, ur, ir, or even or. (Note: They all sound about the same, but are spelled differently.)

V

Tips for Decoding Words with More than One Word Part or Syllable

Big words don't have to be difficult: Bigger words must be broken into smaller parts to be decoded, for example, kitten. If a word has double consonants, divide between double consonants like in kit/ten. If a word has two consonants side by side, for example, admit (ad/mit), divide between the consonants and follow basic long- and short-vowel rules. Other examples are kid/ney, ex/plain, con/crete, and ad/vice.

Note: Blends are generally not divided, for example, scat/ter. Do not break up the (sc) blend. Divide between the two (t's) and use the r-controlled sound.

Vowels and Their Sounds
Long/Short and Controlled by (r)

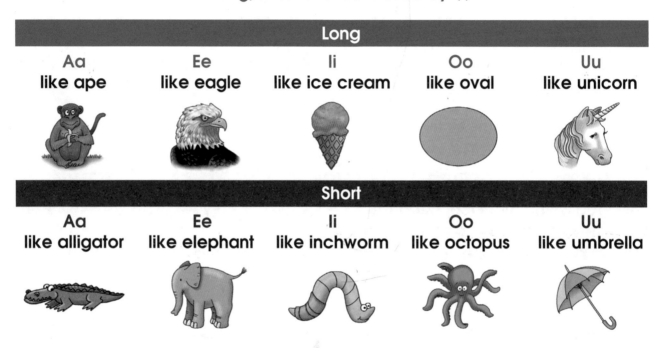

Long				
Aa like ape	Ee like eagle	Ii like ice cream	Oo like oval	Uu like unicorn

Short				
Aa like alligator	Ee like elephant	Ii like inchworm	Oo like octopus	Uu like umbrella

Note: The vowel (Aa) makes three sounds: (long Aa), (short Aa), and the (uh) sound as in (short u). Examples include the following: away, ago, affectionate, ahead, about, agree, afraid, among, around, awake, and awhile.

R – controlled

ar = r like in car

er = er like in fern

ir = ir like in bird

or = or like in fork

ur = ur like in purse

ar = or like in collar

or = er like in color

Note: (er), (ir), (ur), and occasionally (or) are pronounced the same, but spelled differently.

You know the sound (t) makes and you know the sound (h) makes. Why then does (th) make a sound that doesn't sound like either letter sound?

It is because when (h) is paired with some consonants, something unusual happens. The consonants take on new sounds that don't sound like the letters normally do.

Special Sounds with (h)

sh
as in
sheep

th
as in
thumb

wh
as in
whale

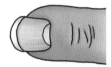

ch
as in
chair

gh
as in
ghost

gh
as in
night

gh
as in
laugh

ph
as in
elephant

Blends
Blends aren't tricky because the letters sound like they should.
What are blends?
Blends are two consonants that are sounded together, but you can hear each letter in the pair.

The most common are the (l), (r), and (s) blends. Blends are found in the beginning, middle, and end of words.

A list of blends follows: br, cr, dr, fr, gr, pr, tr, bl, cl, fl, gl, pl, sc, scr, sk, sl, sm, sn, sp, spl, spr, sq, str, and sw. (tw is another, less common blend.)

Individual Word Group Lists

Word Group 1
father
out
your
friend
picture
zoo
full
poor
give
pretty

Word Group 2
draw
once
would
every
only
write
around
our
you
family

Word Group 3
again
guess
story
all
have
talk
always
house
the
animal

Word Group 4
answer
how
their
any
kind
there
are
know
they
eye
about

Word Group 5
find
good
great
put
said
saw
says
school
shoes
soon

Word Group 6
brother
mother
want
buy
move
was
by
my
watch
circle

Word Group 7
as
laugh
to
away
lion
too
food
look
took
ball

Word Group 8
do
oh
where
does
of
who
down
old
won
one

Word Group 9
lose
through
because
love
very
book
many
walk
both
money

Word Group 10
climb
new
water
color
now
were
come
some
what
could

Code

Use the animal code to figure out the words below.

a alligator	b bear	c cat	d dog	e elephant	f frog	g goat	h horse	i inchworm
j jaguar	k koala	l ladybug	m monkey	n newt	o octopus	p pig	q quail	r rabbit
s skunk	t tiger	u unicorn	v vulture	w walrus	x xenops	y yak	z zebra	

Word Bank

father   out
your   give
zoo   full
poor   friend
picture   pretty

1. ___ ___ ___ ___

2. ___ ___ ___

3. ___ ___ ___ ___ ___ ___ ___

4. ___ ___ ___

5. ___ ___ ___ ___

6. ___ ___ ___ ___ ___ ___

Trace/Build/Write

Trace.

give

Build the word.

Be a Letter Detective. Hunt for the letters that make up the word. Use newspapers, catalogs, or magazines. Cut the letters and glue them in order in the space provided.

Write the word.

Hidden Picture

Pretty Butterfly

Pretty butterfly in the air, your wings are as soft as silk. Pretty butterfly with so many colors, I like the way you look. Pretty butterfly in the air, I wish that I could flutter just the way that you do. Then I would fly away with you.

Follow the Color Code to see what is hidden in the picture.

Color Code
poor = orange
picture = red
put = yellow
pretty = blue

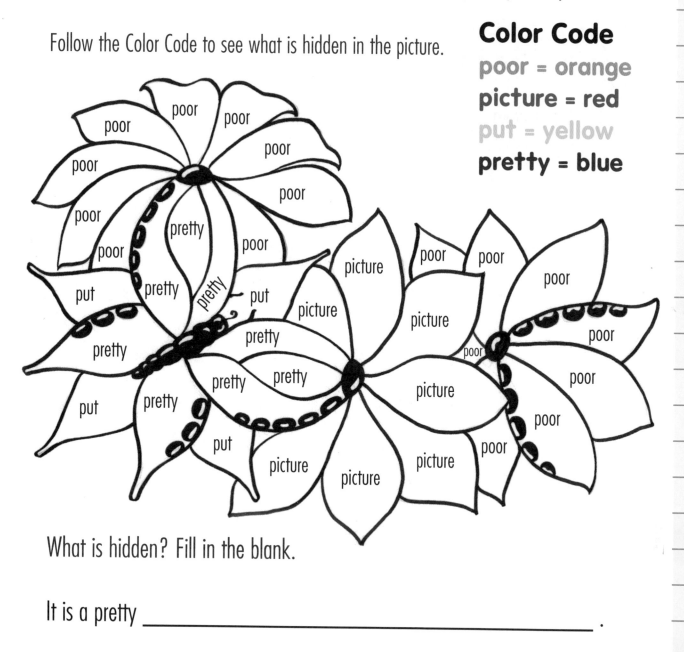

What is hidden? Fill in the blank.

It is a pretty _____ .

Grid

Use the Word Grid to answer the questions.

	A	B	C	D
1	poor	friend	picture	out
2	friend	out	poor	friend
3	out	picture	friend	poor
4	picture	poor	out	picture

1. What word is at B2 on the grid?

2. What word is at D3 on the grid?

3. What word is at A4 on the grid?

4. What word is at C1 on the grid?

5. What word is at B3 on the grid?

6. What word is at A1 on the grid?

7. What word is at C4 on the grid?

8. What word is at D2 on the grid?

9. Use the word at A4, C1, and B3 to fill in the blank:

I will give a pretty _____ to my friend.

10. Use the word at D3 and A1 to fill in the blank:

Father can help the _____ lost kitten.

11. Use the word at B2 and C4 to fill in the blank:

"Time to clean _____ your desk," said Miss Smith.

4 **Word Group 1**

Maze

Help the bear cub find its mother. Which path does the little cub need to take to find its mother? Color the rocks with the word **friend** written on them.

Write the word that names the correct path.

Circle the Picture

Which picture shows something full?
Circle the correct answer.

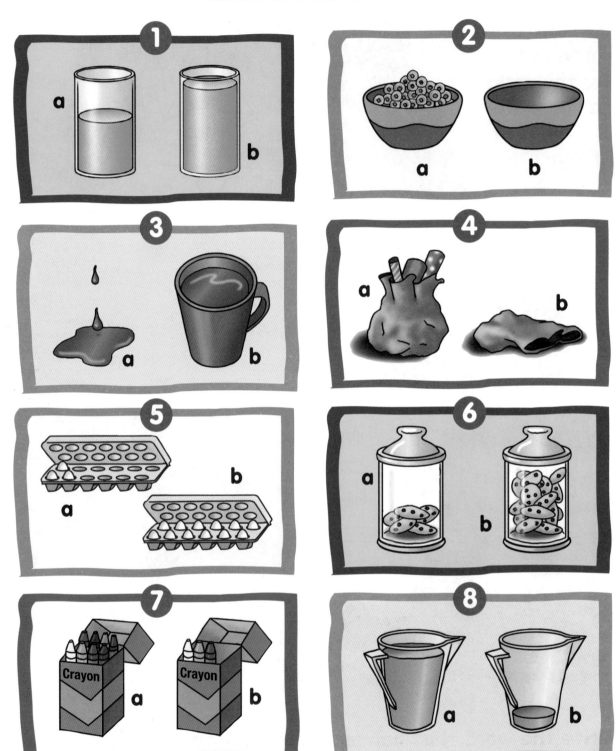

Word Search

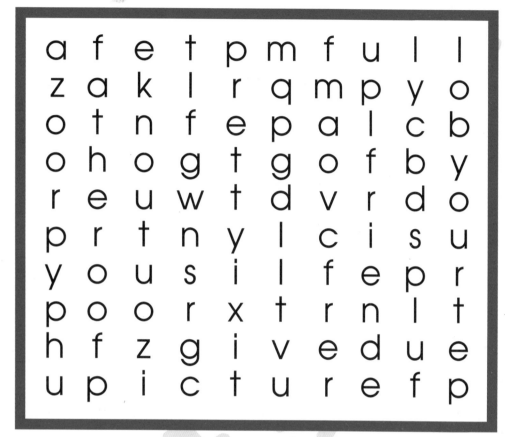

```
a f e t p m f u l l
z a k l r q m p y o
o t n f e p a l c b
o h o g t g o f b y
r e u w t d v r d o
p r t n y l c i s u
y o u s i l f e p r
p o o r x t r n l t
h f z g i v e d u e
u p i c t u r e f p
```

Use the Word Bank to fill in the blanks.

1. Kim is my best_____.

2. I made a _____ picture.

3. I like to _____gifts.

4. The _____ dog had no bones to eat.

Word Bank

give	poor
zoo	out
pretty	father
picture	your
friend	full

Crossword Puzzle

Across
3. a word for dad
7. a drawing or a photo
8. not mine
9. a place for animals

Down
1. hand over
2. not empty
3. a pal
4. not in
5. not rich
6. not ugly

Word Bank
give   poor
zoo   out
pretty   father
picture your
friend   full

Word Group 1

Story Reading

A Trip to the Zoo

Jess went to the **zoo** with her **father**. "The **zoo** is a fun place," said Jess. "I like the things we got to see."

"Your gram is on her way over," said **Father**. "You can share your **trip** to the **zoo** with her."

"I am going to make a **picture** for her," said Jess.

"She will like that," said **Father**.

Jess got **out** her sketch pad. She made a **picture** for Gram. But she did not stop. She made **picture** after **picture**. She worked and worked until her sketch pad was **full**.

"Jess," said **Father**. "Take a time out. **Your poor** hand needs a rest."

"My hand is tired," said Jess. "I will stop and take a rest."

Jess smiled at her **father**. "Here, Dad, I made this **pretty picture** just for you."

"Thank you!" said **Father**. "I like it. Let's put it here." As **Father** hung up the picture, he asked, "Which **picture** will you **give** to Gram?"

"I made this **picture** for Gram," said Jess. "She will like it. She likes birds. I am going to **give** my **friend** Kim a **picture** and my **friend** Zack a **picture**. I am going to keep the rest to help me think of my trip to the **zoo**."

Just then the bell rang.

"Gram is here!" yelled Jess.

"You can share **your** sketches with Gram," said **Father**. "They will help you to think of a lot of things you got to see on your trip to the **zoo**."

Word Group 1 9

Sequencing and ABC Order

Based on the story you just read, put the sentences in logical order from 1 (the first) to 5 (the last).

_____ "Here, Dad, I made this pretty picture just for you."

_____ Jess got out her sketch pad.

_____ Jess went to the zoo with her father.

_____ I am going to keep the rest to help me think of my trip to the zoo.

_____ She made a picture for Gram.

Word Bank

out
picture
zoo
father
pretty

Put these words in ABC order:

your
father
poor
out
give
zoo

1. _____
2. _____
3. _____
4. _____
5. _____
6. _____

Put Word Group 1 in ABC order:

your father poor out give
zoo picture pretty friend full

1. _____
2. _____
3. _____
4. _____
5. _____
6. _____
7. _____
8. _____
9. _____
10. _____

10 **Word Group 1**

Code

Use the animal code to figure out the words below.

1. __ __ __ __

2. __ __ __ __ __

3. __ __ __ __ __ __

4. __ __ __ __ __

5. __ __ __

6. __ __ __ __

Word Bank

draw	write
once	around
would	our
every	you
only	family

Word Group 2 11

Trace/Build/Write

Trace.

once

Build the word.

Be a Letter Detective. Hunt for the letters that make up the word. Use newspapers, catalogs, or magazines. Cut the letters and glue them in order in the space provided.

o n c e

Write the word.

Hidden Picture

Write

I like to write. I can write my name. I can write my letters. I can write my numbers, too. The thing I like to write the best is "I love you."

Follow the Color Code to see what is hidden in the picture.

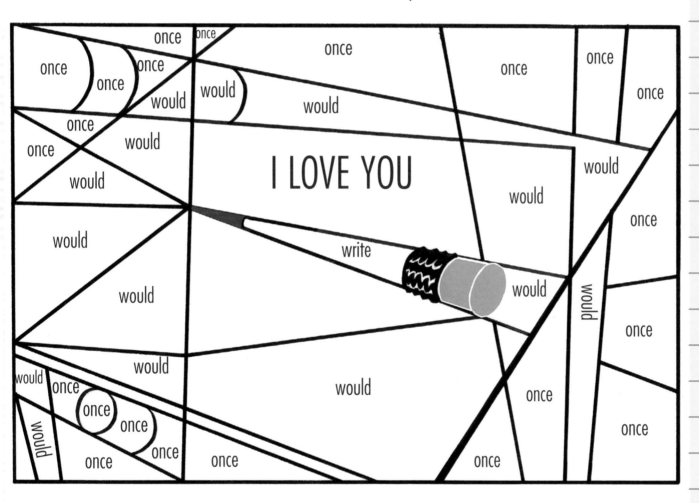

Color Code

write = yellow

once = light green

would = brown

Grid

Use the Word Grid to answer the questions.

	A	B	C	D
1	family	our	every	you
2	our	every	you	family
3	every	you	family	our
4	you	family	our	every

1. What word is at A4 on the grid?

2. What word is at D3 on the grid?

3. What word is at B1 on the grid?

4. What word is at C4 on the grid?

5. What word is at A3 on the grid?

6. What word is at B4 on the grid?

7. What word is at D1 on the grid?

8. What word is at C2 on the grid?

9. Use the word at A4, D1, and C2 to fill in the blank:

_____ did it!

Maze

Help Sam and Ann find their family. Find the path that leads them to their mother, father, and sister. Color the sidewalk blocks that have the word FAMILY on them.

Which of the words on the sidewalk blocks fills in the blank?

We are a happy _____.

Circle the Picture

What can go around?
Circle the correct answer.

Word Group 2

Word Search

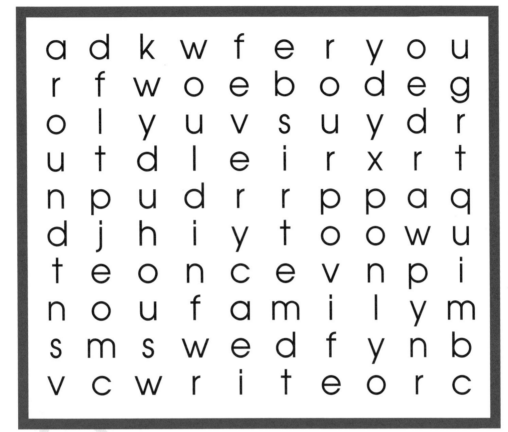

```
a d k w f e r y o u
r f w o e b o d e g
o l y u v s u y d r
u t d l e i r x r t
n p u d r r p p a q
d j h i y t o o w u
t e o n c e v n p i
n o u f a m i l y m
s m s w e d f y n b
v c w r i t e o r c
```

Use the Word Bank to fill in the blanks.

1. I can _____ my name.

2. The hands on a clock go _____.

3. This is the _____ dime I have.

4. Tim likes to_____ pictures.

Crossword Puzzle

Word Bank

write	every
draw	would
only	once
around	you
family	our

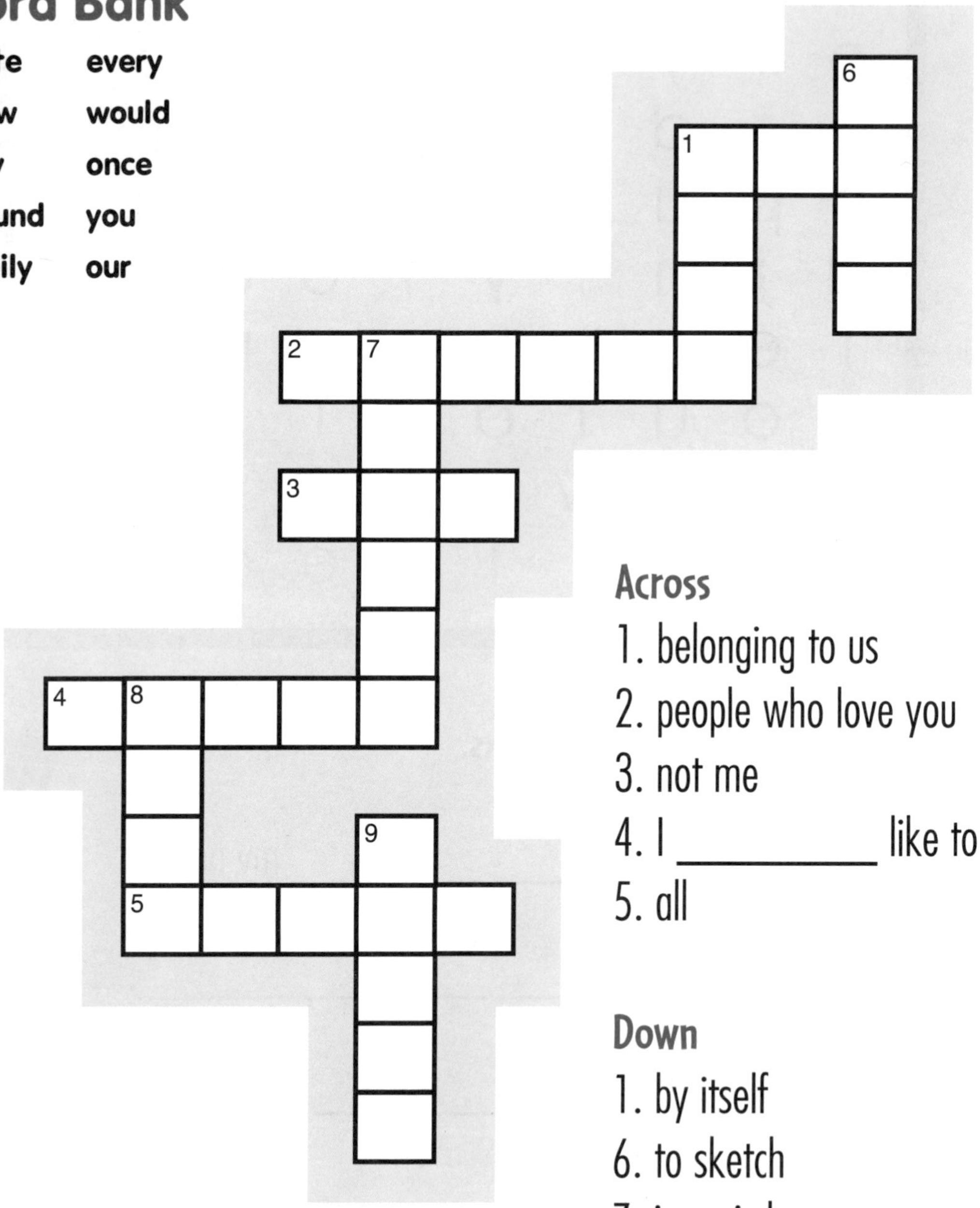

Across

1. belonging to us
2. people who love you
3. not me
4. I _____ like to go.
5. all

Down

1. by itself
6. to sketch
7. in a circle
8. one time
9. to put down letters

Word Group 2

Story Reading

Going Around

Every year Ron and his **family** go on a trip.

"Ron, **would** you like to go to Kidsland Park for **our** summer trip?" asked Mom.

"Yes!" said Ron. "Kidsland Park is the best park!"

"**You** can ride lots of fun rides. **You** can do and see lots of fun things," said Dad.

"I **would** like to ride things that do not go **around**," said Ron. "I don't like to go **around** and **around**. Going **around** makes me feel sick."

"Me, too," said Mom. "I do not like to spin **around**."

"I like the Spin-A-Whirl," said Dad. "It is the best ride at the park. But I am the **only** one that likes to spin **around**. It seems I am going to have to ride those rides without **you** and Mom. That will not be much fun."

"But Dad," said Ron. "The Spin-A-Whirl goes so fast."

"Just ride it **once** with me, Ron. Please?" begged Dad. "Just **once**?"

"Dad!" said Ron. "I think it will make me sick."

Dad turned to Mom, "Well, will **you** ride it with me?" he asked.

"That ride is not for me," said Mom.

"I think the two of **you** need to **write** your names on a slip of paper and I will **draw** a name," said Dad. "The name I **draw** has to ride the Spin-A-Whirl with me. **Once** I **draw** your name, **you** have to ride it. No backing out."

"No way!" said Mom.

"No way!" said Ron.

Dad smiled. "It's a joke," he said. "I do not like to ride rides that spin. But it was fun getting the two of **you** going **around** and **around**."

Word Group 2 19

Sequencing and ABC Order

Based on the story you just read, put the sentences in logical order from 1 (the first) to 5 (the last).

_____ Dad smiled. "It's a joke," he said. "I do not like to ride rides that spin. But it was fun getting the two of you going around and around."

_____ "I would like to ride things that do not go around," said Ron. "Me too," said Mom.

_____ "Ron, would you like to go to Kidsland Park for our summer trip?" asked Mom.

_____ "Just ride it once with me, Ron. Please?" begged Dad.

_____ "Once I draw your name, you have to ride it."

Word Bank

draw

around

once

would

you

Put these words in ABC order:

draw	1. _____	4. _____
around		
family	2. _____	5. _____
you		
every	3. _____	6. _____
write		

Challenge

Put Word Group 2 in ABC order:

write draw you every family
around our once would only

1. _____   6. _____

2. _____   7. _____

3. _____   8. _____

4. _____   9. _____

5. _____   10. _____

Word Group 2

Code

Use the animal code to figure out the words below.

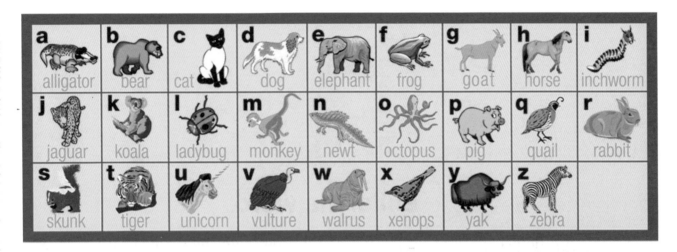

1. ___ ___ ___ ___ ___

2. ___ ___ ___ ___ ___

3. ___ ___ ___ ___ ___

4. ___ ___ ___ ___ ___ ___

5. ___ ___ ___ ___

6. ___ ___ ___ ___ ___ ___

Word Bank

again	guess
story	all
have	talk
always	house
the	animal

Word Group 3   21

Trace/Build/Write

Trace.

the

Build the word.

Be a Letter Detective. Hunt for the letters that make up the word. Use newspapers, catalogs, or magazines. Cut the letters and glue them in order in the space provided.

t   h   e

Write the word.

_____

- - - - - - - - - - - - - - -

_____

Write a sentence on the lines to tell about the picture.

Use <u>The</u> or <u>the</u> in the sentence.

_____

_____

_____

Hidden Picture

I can be big. I can be small. I keep you safe and warm. What am I?

Follow the Color Code to see what is hidden in the picture.

Color Code
full = blue
you = gray
out = green
* = red

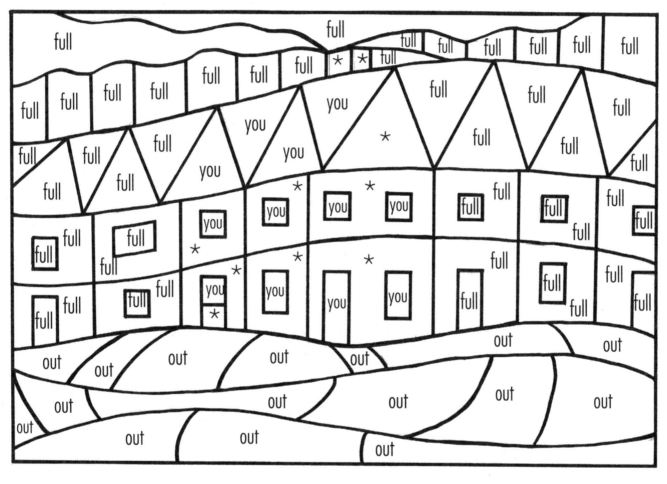

Write the word for what is hidden in the picture.

Write a sentence using the word. _____

_____

_____

Grid

Use the Word Grid to answer the questions.

	A	B	C	D
1	talk	the	have	all
2	have	all	talk	the
3	the	talk	all	have
4	all	have	the	talk

1. What word is at A4 on the grid?

2. What word is at C3 on the grid?

3. What word is at B4 on the grid?

4. What word is at D2 on the grid?

5. What word is at A1 on the grid?

6. What word is at B2 on the grid?

7. What word is at C4 on the grid?

8. What word is at D1 on the grid?

9.   Use the word at A4, C3, and B2 to fill in the blank:

I did them _____ .

10.   Use the words at D2 and C4 to fill in the blank:

I can fill in _____ blank.

11.   Use the word at B4 to fill in the blank:

_____ fun doing the next page.

Maze

Help the lost animals find their way back to the zoo. Follow the path that is marked with the word pattern <u>again</u>, <u>all</u>, <u>have</u>, <u>talk</u>. Draw a line to mark the correct path.

Circle the Picture

Circle each animal you see in the picture.

monkey bird **porcupine** lion **elephant** fish
iguana **giraffe** ostrich turtle

Word Search

```
g m e d s z s o a y
u a t a l k t n l c
e g h b q s o l w k
s a e f v c r j a g
s i h q w l y e y a
o n y u e h o u s e
t a n i m a l i v a
y m t h a v f t a l
e r e d n e s d m l
a n x c v k p i r w
```

Use the Word Bank to fill in the blanks.

Word Bank

again	talk
guess	always
story	house
all	the
have	animal

1. A dog is an_____.

2. The girl lives in a _____ on Hill Street.

3. Can you _____ what is in the box?

4. The note said, "Love _____, Tim."

Word Group 3 27

Crossword Puzzle

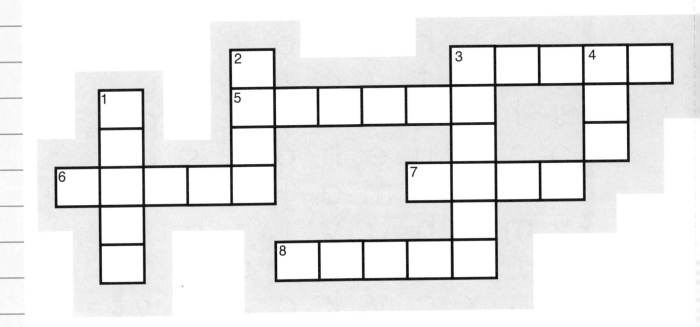

Across

3. once more
5. a dog, a cat, a pig
6. a place to live
7. speak
8. a chance answer

Down

1. a tale
2. I _____ a pet.
3. every time
4. every one

Word Bank

guess   all   have   story   always

house   again   animal   talk

Story Reading

A Brand New Story

Mr. Tweed and his wife woke up on Saturday.

"Saturday is our day for yard work," said Mrs. Tweed.

Mr. Tweed **always** cut **the** grass. Mrs. Tweed **always** pulled **the** weeds. Every Saturday it was **the** same **story**.

"Yes, I see it's Saturday **again**," said Mr. Tweed. "It is time to make **the** yard neat."

"**The house always** looks pretty when **the** grass is cut and **the** weeds are pulled," said Mrs. Tweed.

"I **guess** we better get to work," said Mr. Tweed.

Mr. Tweed cut and cut, and Mrs. Tweed pulled and pulled. **The** sun rose high in **the** sky. Mr. and Mrs. Tweed began to get hot. Mr. and Mrs. Tweed stopped working for **the** day.

"**All** that work has made me hot and tired. I **have** to sit," said Mrs. Tweed.

"I am hot and tired just **the** same as you," said Mr. Tweed. "Let's sit in **the** shade. We will **talk** and rest."

Mr. and Mrs. Tweed sat on **the** porch swing. A bird perched on a branch and sang them a song. A cricket hopped up on **the** porch and chimed in with a scritch, scritch, scritch, and a kitten slinked up with a meow, meow.

"Listen to each **animal** as it sings," said Mrs. Tweed.

"It seems **the** animals **have** gathered to tell us a **story** and sing us a song," said Mr. Tweed.

Mrs. Tweed replied, "I'm glad we stopped to hear them tell us a brand new **story** and sing their pretty tune."

Sequencing and ABC Order

Based on the story you just read, put the sentences in logical order from 1 (the first) to 5 (the last).

_____ "All that work has made me hot and tired. I have to sit," said Mrs. Tweed.

_____ The sun rose high in the sky.

_____ "I'm glad we stopped to hear them tell us a brand new story and sing their pretty tune."

_____ "I guess we better get to work," said Mr. Tweed.

_____ "The house always looks pretty when the grass is cut and the weeds are pulled," said Mrs. Tweed.

Word Bank

The
guess
story
All
house

Put these words in ABC order:

the
guess
story
all
house

1. _____   4. _____

2. _____   5. _____

3. _____

Challenge

Put Word Group 3 in ABC order:

again guess story all have
talk always house the animal

1. _____   6. _____

2. _____   7. _____

3. _____   8. _____

4. _____   9. _____

5. _____   10. _____

Word Group 3

Code

Use the animal code to figure out the words below.

a alligator	b bear	c cat	d dog	e elephant	f frog	g goat	h horse	i inchworm
j jaguar	k koala	l ladybug	m monkey	n newt	o octopus	p pig	q quail	r rabbit
s skunk	t tiger	u unicorn	v vulture	w walrus	x xenops	y yak	z zebra	

Word Bank

answer   how
their   any
kind   there
are   know
they   eye
about

1. ____ ____ ____ ____

2. ____ ____ ____

3. ____ ____ ____ ____ ____ ____

4. ____ ____ ____ ____ ____

5. ____ ____ ____ ____ ____

6. ____ ____ ____

Trace/Build/Write

Trace.

they

Build the word.

Be a Letter Detective. Hunt for the letters that make up the word. Use newspapers, catalogs, or magazines. Cut the letters and glue them in order in the space provided.

t h e y

Write the word.

Hidden Picture

One Eye or Two Eyes
One eye, two eyes, what do you see?
I see sand and the deep blue sea.
One eye, two eyes, what do you see?
I see boats. There are one, two, three!

Follow the Color Code to see what is hidden in the picture.

Color Code
eye = pink
how = orange
any = light blue
are = dark blue
all = light green
the = light brown
out = yellow

Grid

Use the Word Grid to answer the questions.

	A	B	C	D
1	are	they	how	know
2	they	are	know	how
3	how	know	are	they
4	know	how	they	are

1. What word is at C4 on the grid?

2. What word is at B3 on the grid?

3. What word is at A1 on the grid?

4. What word is at D2 on the grid?

5. What word is at A4 on the grid?

6. What word is at D3 on the grid?

7. What word is at C1 on the grid?

8. What word is at B2 on the grid?

9. Use the word at B3 and A4 to fill in the blank:

You _____ them all.

10. Use the word at A1 and B2 to fill in the blank:

You _____ so smart!

Maze

There — a place

Their — belonging to

From Here to There

Read each sentence. Which form of <u>there</u>/<u>their</u> is correct for the sentence? Circle the correct answer for each question. Then look at the picture below. Check the paths to see which one has the answers you chose. Color the path that has the correct answers for 1–10. Which path of stepping-stones will get you across the river safely?

1. The books are (there, their) in the stack.

2. (There, Their) house is big.

3. The dog is (there, their) pet.

4. Set the drink (there, their).

5. I like to go (there, their) to play.

6. I like to see (there, their) drawings.

7. How did (there, their) team do?

8. I can sit (there, their).

9. Can you guess (there, their) size?

10. Please stand (there, their) and wait.

Circle the Picture

Which picture shows something kind happening?
Circle the correct answer.

Word Group 4

Word Search

```
t h e r e a b o u t
s n b i d s h d k a
a q a r s t o t n r
n r w k a h w u o e
y p t i u e v l w o
j l g n y i f e j n
h o e d m r g y i y
r p q s g h x e o r
w t h e y w q r z t
e n f l a n s w e r
m h i o c e l d k s
```

Use the Word Bank to fill in the blanks.

1. Can you _____ the problems?

2. Are _____ hard?

3. I bet you _____ how to do them!

Word Bank

answer	how
their	any
kind	there
are	know
they	eye
about	

Word Group 4   37

Crossword Puzzle

Word Bank

how	they	kind	about
eye	answer	any	there
know	their	are	

Across

1. a word that sounds like no but isn't spelled the same
2. reply to a question
4. all of them
5. one of
7. a place

Down

1. nice, polite
2. What is the story_____?
3. _____ are you feeling?
4. belonging to them
5. We _____ friends.
6. used for seeing

Story Reading

Getting the Eye

Quinn and Jake went to the Fine Arts Center. Jake held the map.

"Let's go in this room first," he said. "It is called the Portrait Room."

They went in. "Look, **there are** all **kinds** of people on the wall in here," said Quinn. "They seem to be keeping **their eye** on us. Every time I turn around, they are staring back."

"That's silly," said Jake as he kept his **eye** on the map. "Paintings can't stare."

"I **know**," said Quinn. "But just look around the room once and you will see."

Jake scanned the room, and to his surprise more than one painting seemed to stare back.

"Do you see **how their** eyes stare?" asked Quinn.

Jake and Quinn felt scared. "Yes, let's get the clerk," said Jake. "I need to **know** more **about** these strange paintings. I need an **answer about how** paintings can stare. I **know there** must be a reason for it. **Any answer** will help make me feel better."

Jake and Quinn came back with the clerk. The clerk explained that artists use tricks to make paintings look as if they are looking at you.

"**They** make you feel like you are in the painting," she said. Before she left the room, she added with a smile, "Did the paintings scare you? You need to stop seeing scary TV shows. You are both acting jumpy."

Quinn and Jake smiled. **They** were happy to **know** the **answer about how** paintings can stare. **They** looked in every room of the Fine Arts Center. **They** had a super time looking at all the forms of art.

The next day in art class **their** teacher, Mr. Hartnett, had them make portrait paintings. Quinn and Jake worked hard on **their** portraits. The students in **their** class liked **how they** made **their** paintings give them the **eye**.

Word Group 4 39

Sequencing and ABC Order

Based on the story you just read, put the sentences in logical order from 1 (the first) to 5 (the last).

Word Bank

eye

their

are

how

know

_____ The next day in art class their teacher, Mr. Hartnett, had them make portrait paintings.

_____ "They seem to be keeping their eye on us."

_____ The students in their class liked how they made their paintings give them the eye.

_____ "Look, there are all kinds of people on the wall in here," said Quinn.

_____ "Yes, let's get the clerk," said Jake. "I need to know more about these strange paintings."

Put these words in ABC order:

answer
kind
how
they
eye

1. _____   4. _____

2. _____   5. _____

3. _____

Challenge

Put Word Group 4 in ABC order:

answer how their any kind
there are know they eye about

1. _____   7. _____
2. _____   8. _____
3. _____   9. _____
4. _____   10. _____
5. _____   11. _____
6. _____

 40 Word Group 4

Code

Use the animal code to figure out the words below.

a alligator	**b** bear	**c** cat	**d** dog	**e** elephant	**f** frog	**g** goat	**h** horse	**i** inchworm
j jaguar	**k** koala	**l** ladybug	**m** monkey	**n** newt	**o** octopus	**p** pig	**q** quail	**r** rabbit
s skunk	**t** tiger	**u** unicorn	**v** vulture	**w** walrus	**x** xenops	**y** yak	**z** zebra	

1. ___ ___ ___

2. ___ ___ ___ ___

3. ___ ___ ___ ___ ___

4. ___ ___ ___ ___

5. ___ ___ ___ ___

6. ___ ___ ___

Word Bank

find	good
great	put
said	saw
says	school
shoes	soon

Word Group 5 41

Trace/Build/Write

Trace.

said

Build the word.

Be a Letter Detective. Hunt for the letters that make up the word. Use newspapers, catalogs, or magazines. Cut the letters and glue them in order in the space provided.

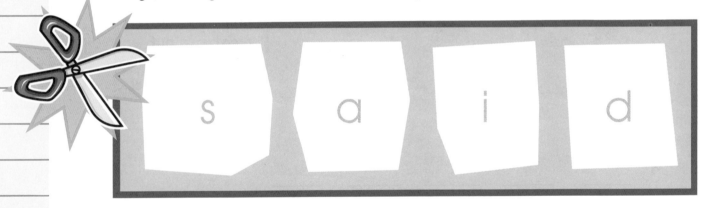

s   a   i   d

Write the word.

_____

- - - - - - - - - - - - - - - - - -

_____

The word said is used to tell what someone had to say. These marks " " show what someone said.

1. Mom said, "Go to bed."
   "Go to bed," said Mom.
   Write what Mom said.

2. Write your name in the blank.
   "This is fun!" said _____.

Hidden Picture

You work there. You play there.
You make friends there. You eat there.
You sing there. Where is there?
Find the answer in the picture.

Color Code

school = light blue
shoes = light green
soon = dark green
saw = red
says = gray
said = light brown

Follow the Color Code to see what is hidden in the picture.

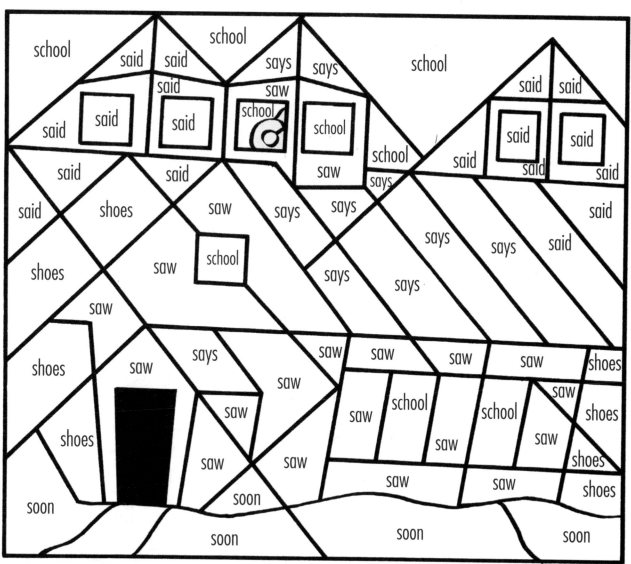

Write the answer to the riddle.

Grid

Use the Word Grid to answer the questions.

	A	B	C	D
1	great	says	saw	put
2	put	saw	says	great
3	saw	put	great	says
4	says	great	put	saw

1. What word is at C4 on the grid?

2. What word is at C3 on the grid?

3. What word is at D1 on the grid?

4. What word is at A2 on the grid?

5. What word is at B2 on the grid?

6. What word is at D4 on the grid?

7. What word is at B1 on the grid?

8. What word is at A3 on the grid?

9. Use the word at C4, D1, and A2 to fill in the blank:

_____ **your name on your paper.**

10. Use the word at B2, D4, and A3 to fill in the blank:

I _____ you at the park.

11. Use the word at C3 to fill in the blank:

You did a _____ job!

44 Word Group 5

Maze

Help Sue, Kim, and Don find their way to school. They must follow the path that has the words great and good written in a repeated pattern. Color the sidewalk blocks with great and good written in a pattern that repeats.

great
good
great

| soon | saw | good |
| find | said | great |

| said | good | good | saw |
| find | great | said | great |

| good | find | saw | great |
| soon | great | soon | said |

| good | find | great |
| great | soon | good |

Use the words great and good to fill in the blanks.
You did a

job!
You did a

job!
You did a super job! You are so smart!

Circle the Picture

Circle the shoes that answer the question.

1. I can run in this shoe.

2. I can tap in this shoe.

3. I can hike in this shoe.

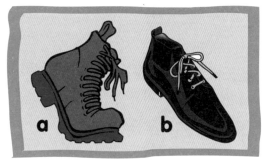

4. I can go to the beach in this shoe.

5. I can look well dressed in this shoe.

6. I can play football in this shoe.

7. I can scuba dive in this shoe.

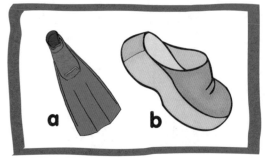

8. I can do hard work in this shoe.

Word Search

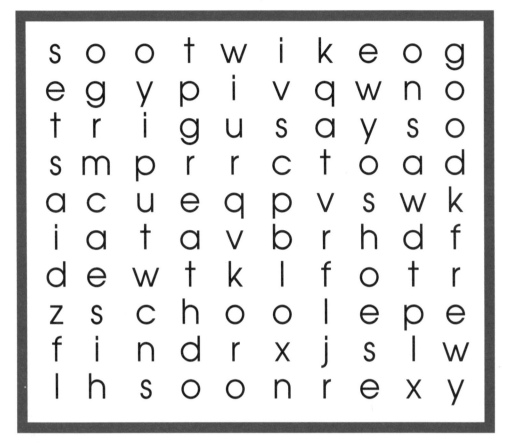

```
s o o t w i k e o g
e g y p i v q w n o
t r i g u s a y s o
s m p r r c t o a d
a c u e q p v s w k
i a t a v b r h d f
d e w t k l f o t r
z s c h o o l e p e
f i n d r x j s l w
l h s o o n r e x y
```

Word Bank

find	good
great	put
said	saw
says	school
shoes	soon

Use the Word Bank to fill in the blanks.

1. I _____ a bug yesterday.

2. Dad will be home _____.

3. "I can help you," _____ the clerk.

4. _____ the bags here, please.

Crossword Puzzle

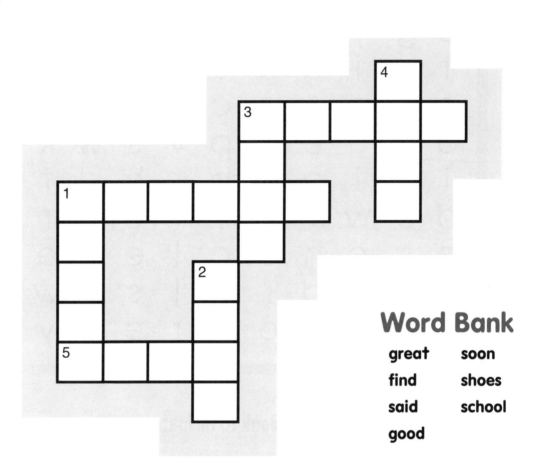

Word Bank

great	soon
find	shoes
said	school
good	

Across

1. a place to learn
3. more than usual, much
5. in a short time

Down

1. worn on the feet
2. to see what is hidden
3. The class did a

_____ job.

4. spoke

Story Reading

With Fingers Crossed

Back To School Sale!

Jen came to see Cam. Cam **saw** Jen ride her bike up to the house. Cam ran to see Jen. She had an ad from the paper in her hand.

"Look, Cam!" **said** Jen. "The ad **says**, 'Don't miss Vick's Back to **School** Sale.'"

"That's **great**!" **said** Cam.

"Vick's Clothing Store has the best school clothes!" **said** Jen. "Do you think you can come to Vick's with my family and me?"

"I will have to ask my mom," **said** Cam. "Just last week my mother **said** I need a little bit of everything: **shoes**, pants, shirts, and underclothes. If I am able to go, I can see what I like. Then my mom can take me shopping later."

"I hope we **find good** deals on clothes," **said** Jen. "My mom likes when there are sales. She always lets me get a toy if she gets **good** deals."

"I hope my mom says I can go. It will be fun shopping for clothes. Plus, I hope your mom will **find great** sales so she will take us toy shopping," **said** Cam.

"I would like to find a **good** game," **said** Jen.

"I **put** the cash I got for my birthday in my piggy bank and have been saving it to get a nice toy. I can't wait to see all the neat stuff. I'll go in and ask if I can go with you. I will be out **soon**," **said** Cam.

"**Great**!" **said** Jen. "I'll wait with my fingers crossed."

In a flash Cam came out.

"I can go!" **said** Cam. "I can't wait to get to Vick's. Now it's my turn to cross my fingers. I hope your mom gets **great** deals so we can shop for toys."

Word Group 5 49

Sequencing and ABC Order

Based on the story you just read, put the sentences in logical order from 1 (the first) to 5 (the last).

_____ "I can go!" said Cam. "I can't wait to get to Vick's."

_____ Cam saw Jen ride her bike up to the house.

_____ "Just last week my mother said I need a little bit of everything: shoes, pants, shirts, and underclothes."

_____ "I'll go in and ask if I can go with you. I will be out soon," said Cam.

_____ "Look, Cam!" said Jen. "The ad says, 'Don't miss Vick's Back to School Sale.'"

Word Bank

soon   said

saw   shoes

School

Put these words in ABC order:

put
says
find
great

1. _____   3. _____

2. _____   4. _____

Challenge

Put Word Group 5 in ABC order:

find good soon said put saw
says school great shoes

1. _____   6. _____
2. _____   7. _____
3. _____   8. _____
4. _____   9. _____
5. _____   10. _____

50   **Word Group 5**

Code

Use the animal code to figure out the words below.

1. __ __ __ __

Word Bank

brother	mother
want	buy
move	was
by	my
watch	circle

2. __ __ __

3. __ __ __ __ __ __

4. __ __ __ __

5. __ __ __ __ __ __

6. __ __ __ __ __ __ __

Trace/Build/Write

Trace.

w a s

Build the word.

Be a Letter Detective. Hunt for the letters that make up the word. Use newspapers, catalogs, or magazines. Cut the letters and glue them in order in the space provided.

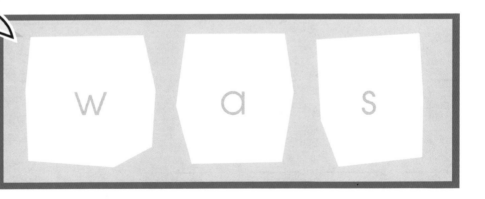

Write the word.

Hidden Picture

Is it a (b) or is it a (d)?

Follow the Color Code to see what is hidden in the picture.

Color Code

b = orange

d = blue

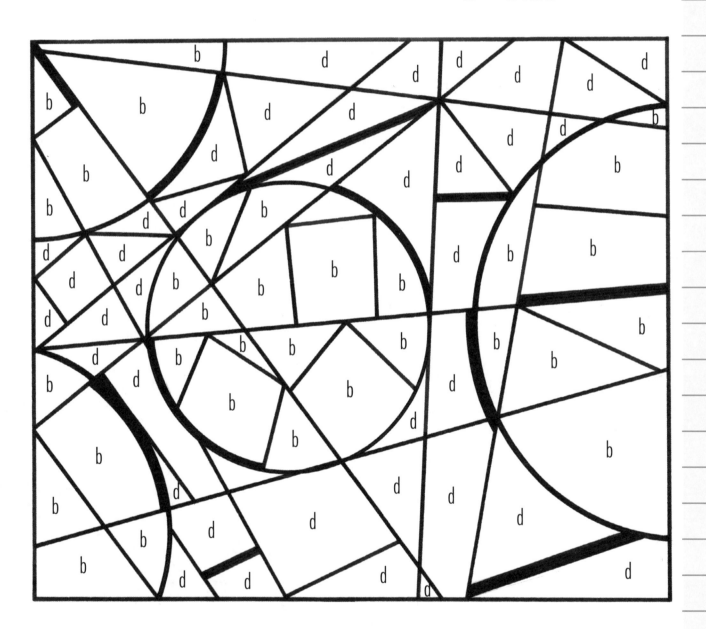

I have no sides. I am a shape. What am I?

Grid

Use the Word Grid to answer the questions.

	A	B	C	D
1	by	watch	buy	my
2	buy	my	watch	by
3	my	buy	by	watch
4	watch	by	my	buy

1. What word is at B4 on the grid?

2. What word is at D1 on the grid?

3. What word is at C3 on the grid?

4. What word is at A2 on the grid?

5. What word is at B1 on the grid?

6. What word is at C4 on the grid?

7. What word is at A3 on the grid?

8. What word is at D2 on the grid?

9. What word is at B4, C3, and D2?

10. What word in D1, C4, and A3 rhymes with answer 9?

Maze

Help Little Brother find Big Brother at the playground. Color the path that leads to the boy's big brother.

Clue: Little Brother has the word buy written on his shirt. His big brother is wearing a shirt with a word that is not spelled the same, but is said just like the word on Little Brother's shirt.

Circle the Picture

What do I want? Circle it.

1. The thing I want has wheels.

2. The thing I want has fur.

3. The thing I want is striped.

4. The thing I want is sweet.

5. The thing I want has gills.

6. The thing I want has a beak.

Draw a picture of something you want.

Write a sentence to go with your picture.

_____

_____

_____

_____

_____

Word Search

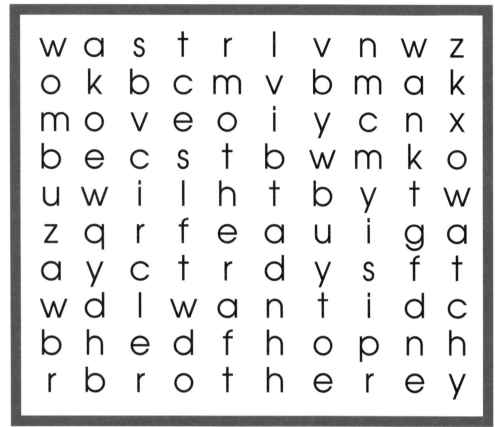

```
w  a  s  t  r  l  v  n  w  z
o  k  b  c  m  v  b  m  a  k
m  o  v  e  o  i  y  c  n  x
b  e  c  s  t  b  w  m  k  o
u  w  i  l  h  t  b  y  t  w
z  q  r  f  e  a  u  i  g  a
a  y  c  t  r  d  y  s  f  t
w  d  l  w  a  n  t  i  d  c
b  h  e  d  f  h  o  p  n  h
r  b  r  o  t  h  e  r  e  y
```

Use the Word Bank to fill in the blanks.

1. A _____ is a shape.

2. A word that means "mom" is _____.

3. You can tell time on a _____.

4. A word that means "to pay for" is _____.

Word Bank

brother
mother
want
buy
move
was
by
my
watch
circle

Crossword Puzzle

Word Bank

mother	want
brother	watch
by	circle
my	was
move	buy

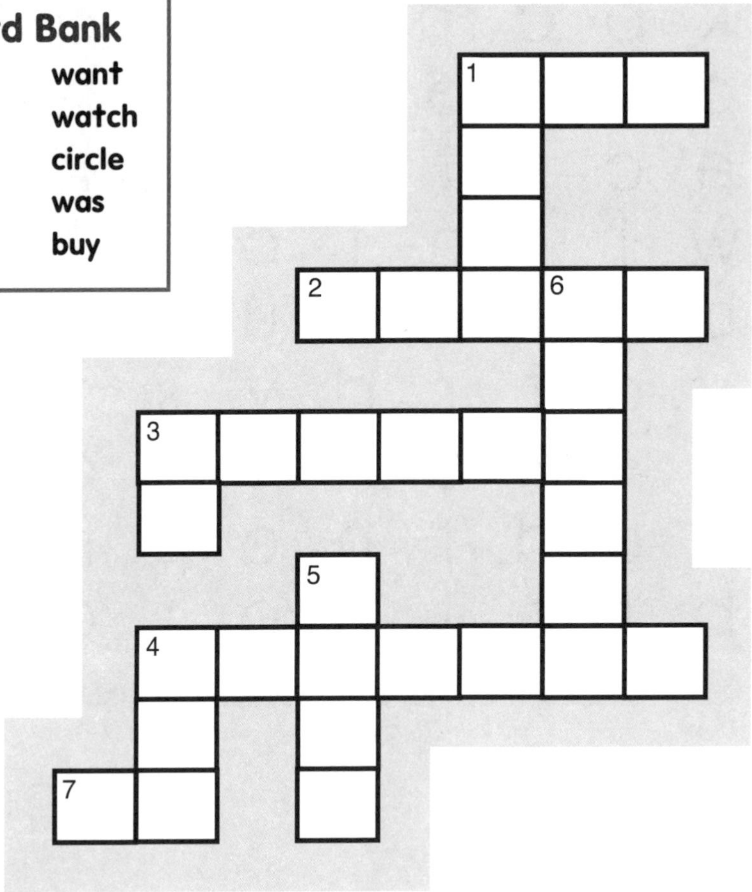

Across

1. He ___________ happy.
2. look at
3. a word that means mom
4. not your sister
7. near

Down

1. wish for
3. belonging to me
4. get by paying a price
5. change place
6. a shape

Story Reading

Family Fun

Devin Zimmer, his **mother**, and his **brother** Smith all liked to play games. They had games of all sorts. It seemed there was not a game they did not like to play.

Mr. Zimmer did not like to play games, but he liked to **buy** games for his family. He liked to **watch** them **move** around the game board, each trying to reach the winner's **circle** first. He liked to hear the boys yell, "Please, let's play again!"

Each time he went shopping, Mr. Zimmer stopped **by** The Game Zone.

He would ask the store's owner, "Which game do you think **my** family would **want** this time?"

The store owner always helped him pick the perfect game.

"Here is a game for you to add to the pile," Mr. Zimmer would say when he got home.

His family would be thrilled. "Good job, Dad!" the boys would yell. "That **was** the game we saw on TV. We have been hoping for it."

"Yes, Dear," his wife would agree. "That looks like a fun game. Great job!"

When people asked if he liked games, Mr. Zimmer would say, "**My** family likes games. I just like to **watch** them have fun."

Sequencing and ABC Order

Based on the story you just read, put the sentences in logical order from 1 (the first) to 5 (the last).

_____ Each time he went shopping, Mr. Zimmer stopped by The Game Zone.

_____ Devin Zimmer, his mother, and his brother Smith all liked to play games.

_____ He liked to watch them move around the game board, each trying to reach the winner's circle first.

_____ When people asked if he liked games, Mr. Zimmer would say, "My family likes games. I just like to watch them have fun."

_____ Mr. Zimmer did not like to play games, but he liked to buy games for his family.

Put these words in ABC order:

was
my
circle
by

1. _____   3. _____

2. _____   4. _____

Challenge

Put Word Group 6 in ABC order:

brother mother want buy
move was by my watch circle

1. _____   6. _____
2. _____   7. _____
3. _____   8. _____
4. _____   9. _____
5. _____   10. _____

Code

Use the animal code to figure out the words below.

1. _____ _____

2. _____ _____ _____ _____

3. _____ _____

4. _____ _____ _____ _____

5. _____ _____ _____ _____

6. _____ _____ _____

Word Bank

as	laugh
to	away
lion	too
food	look
took	ball

Trace/Build/Write

Trace.

laugh

Build the word.

Be a Letter Detective. Hunt for the letters that make up the word.
Use newspapers, catalogs, or magazines. Cut the letters
and glue them in order in the space provided.

l a u g h

Hidden Picture

What is hidden in the picture?

Follow the Color Code to see what is hidden in the picture.

Color Code
L = dark brown
l = yellow
b = light blue
i = green
ll = light brown

Grid

Use the Word Grid to answer the questions.

	A	B	C	D
1	ball	as	to	too
2	as	to	too	ball
3	to	too	ball	as
4	too	ball	as	to

1. What word is at C2 on the grid?

2. What word is at B4 on the grid?

3. What word is at D3 on the grid?

4. What word is at A1 on the grid?

5. What word is at D4 on the grid?

6. What word is at C1 on the grid?

7. What word is at B2 on the grid?

8. What word is at A4 on the grid?

9. Use the word at D4, C1, and B2 to fill in the first blank.
   Use the word at B4 and A1 to fill in the second blank.
   Use the word at C2 and A4 to fill in the third blank.

"I like _____ play _____ ,"said Sam.

"Me, _____ !" said Kim.

Maze

Which way should Lion go to find his friends waiting for him in the jungle? Look at the five-word repeated patterns. Lion should take the path where the first word in the pattern is away and the last word in the five-word repeated pattern is as. Color it.

Circle the Picture

Circle the food you see in the picture.

The food I like best is:

Draw a picture to go with your sentence.

Word Search

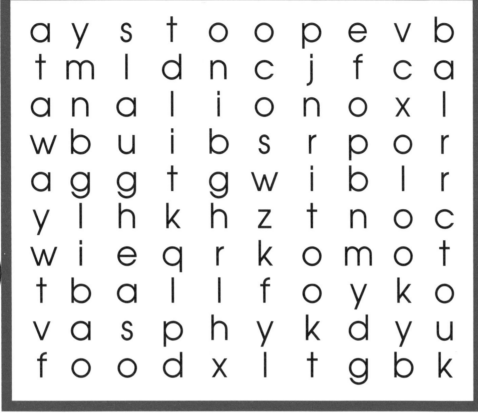

a y s t o o p e v b
t m l d n c j f c a
a n a l i o n o x l
w b u i b s r p o r
a g g t g w i b l r
y l h k h z t n o c
w i e q r k o m o t
t b a l l f o y k o
v a s p h y k d y u
f o o d x l t g b k

Word Bank

as
laugh
to
away
lion
too
food
look
took
ball

Use the Word Bank to fill in the blanks.

1. The _____ is in the cage.

2. It eats a lot of _____.

3. A man _____ the food to him.

4. The man gave him the food and _____ he went.

Crossword Puzzle

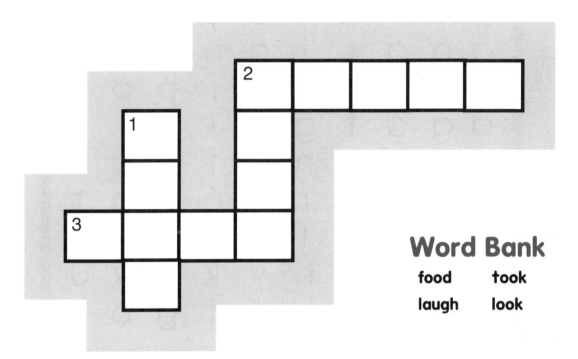

Word Bank

food	took
laugh	look

Across

2. Funny jokes always make me _____.

3. He _____ the dog for a walk.

Down

1. Pizza is my favorite _____.

2. When you cross the street, _____ both ways.

Story Reading

A Friend for Lion

Lion wished for a friend **to** play with. Each day he went **to** the park. Every time he went, he **took** his **ball**.

"Playing **ball** would be more fun if only I had a friend," said **Lion**.

"How I wish I had a friend."

As soon **as** he said his wish, a little bird perched in a tree. He called out **to Lion**. "I hear you would like **to** have a friend," said the little bird. "I **too** am in need of a friend."

"That is great!" said **Lion**. "Would you like to play **ball**?"

"Yes, I would like to play **ball**," said the bird **as** he **took** the **ball** from **Lion**.

"Just look at all the tricks I know," said Bird.

Bird spun the **ball** on his wing. He dribbled the **ball**. He rolled it. He twirled it. He did trick after trick.

Lion began **to** laugh. "I like your tricks. Can you teach me how **to** do all those neat things with a **ball**?" asked **Lion**.

"Yes, I can teach you," said Bird. "We will have great fun!"

Lion and Bird played all day long. They played so long they didn't even stop **to** eat a bite of **food**.

When the sun was just about **to** set, **Lion** and Bird said farewell. They each went **away** smiling, knowing that they had made a friend.

Word Group 7   69

Sequencing and ABC Order

Based on the story you just read, put the sentences in logical order from 1 (the first) to 5 (the last).

_____ "I hear you would like to have a friend," said the little bird.

_____ Lion wished for a friend to play with.

_____ "Can you teach me how to do all those neat things with a ball?" asked Lion.

_____ As soon as he said his wish, a little bird perched in a tree.

_____ They each went away smiling, knowing that they had made a friend.

Word Bank

away

Lion

to

as

ball

Put these words in ABC order:

as
took
laugh
food
ball

1. _____   4. _____

2. _____   5. _____

3. _____

Challenge

Put Word Group 7 in ABC order:

ball took look food too
lion away to laugh as

1. _____   6. _____

2. _____   7. _____

3. _____   8. _____

4. _____   9. _____

5. _____   10. _____

Code

Use the animal code to figure out the words below.

1. _____ _____

2. _____ _____ _____ _____

Word Bank

do	oh
where	does
of	who
down	old
won	one

3. _____ _____

4. _____ _____ _____

5. _____ _____ _____ _____

6. _____ _____ _____ _____ _____

Word Group 8 71

Trace/Build/Write

Trace.

who

Build the word.

Be a Letter Detective. Hunt for the letters that make up the word.
Use newspapers, catalogs, or magazines. Cut the letters
and glue them in order in the space provided.

Write the word.

_____

- -

_____

Hidden Picture

What can it be?

Follow the Color Code to see what is hidden in the picture.

Color Code

1 = orange

2 = yellow

3 = blue

What is hidden in the picture?

Grid

Use the Word Grid to answer the questions.

	A	B	C	D
1	oh	does	of	do
2	does	of	do	oh
3	of	do	oh	does
4	do	oh	does	of

1. What word is at B2 on the grid?

2. What word is at D4 on the grid?

3. What word is at A3 on the grid?

4. What word is at C1 on the grid?

5. What word is at B4 on the grid?

6. What word is at C3 on the grid?

7. What word is at A4 on the grid?

8. What word is at B1 on the grid?

9. What word is at B2, D4, A3, and C1 on the grid?

Maze

Help Kitten find her milk.
Which path does the kitten need to take to get to the milk?
Color the stones with the word does on them.

Circle the Picture

Circle what a boy or girl can do.

Word Search

```
p  w  i  g  v  o  h  b  d  o
g  h  o  h  d  o  k  g  d  v
u  o  p  j  o  s  f  s  w  e
g  r  a  k  e  a  i  w  l  s
o  n  e  l  s  h  o  t  i  x
q  t  s  z  b  q  l  r  f  j
w  y  d  x  n  n  d  s  d  o
d  o  w  n  m  m  y  w  t  o
e  u  f  r  k  c  o  o  p  f
w  h  e  r  e  d  v  n  c  l
```

Word Bank

do	oh
where	does
of	who
down	old
won	one

Use the Word Bank to fill in the blanks.

1. I can go _____ the hill.

2. _____ will come with me?

3. Which _____ of you is brave like me?

Word Group 8 77

Crossword Puzzle

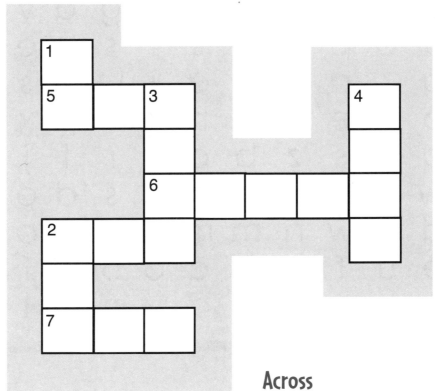

Across

2. I _____ the race.

5. The house is _____.

6. Do you know _____ he lives?

7. I will have just _____ treat.

Down

1. What can we _____?

2. I know _____ it is!

3. I like to go _____ the slide.

4. She _____ her best to win.

Word Bank

does	one
where	do
down	old
who	won

Story Reading

Off to the Races

Tom and Jeff liked to ride bikes. They liked to ride often. One day as they rode, they spotted a path.

"Look! A path," said Tom.

"**Where does** it go?" said Jeff.

"I have no clue," said Tom. "I did not know there was a path there."

"Me, either," said Jeff. "Let's explore!"

The boys parked their bikes and walked **down** the path. As they walked, they saw bushes and vines. Then they saw an **old** shed.

"I know that shed," said Tom. "It belongs to Mr. Kay."

"**Do** you know him?" asked Jeff.

"Not well, but my dad **does**," said Tom. "I met him **one** time. He is the man **who** won all the trophies for car racing."

"**Oh**, I would like to meet him. I am a race fan," said Jeff.

Just then Mr. Kay came riding his bike **down** the path.

"Hello, boys!" he said with a smile. "It is a great day for a bike ride."

"Yes, it is," the boys chimed.

"Do you know me?" asked Tom. "I am Don Parker's son."

"Yes, I do, Tom. You look just like him," said Mr. Kay. "How is your dad?"

"He is fine. This is my friend Jeff. He is a race fan."

"Stop by next Sunday and I will get you boys tickets for next week's race," said Mr. Kay. "It'll be **one of** the best races **of** the season."

"**Oh** boy," said Jeff. "That's great. Thank you!"

"Thank you, Mr. Kay," said Tom.

"You boys have a good day," said Mr. Kay as he waved and rode on **down** the path.

"**Oh**, I can't wait for Sunday," said Jeff.

"Same here," said Tom.

"Yippee!" they shouted. "We're off to the races!"

Word Group 8 79

Sequencing and ABC Order

Based on the story you just read, put the sentences in logical order from 1 (the first) to 5 (the last).

_____ "I know that shed," said Tom. "It belongs to Mr. Kay." "Do you know him?" asked Jeff.

_____ "Look! A path," said Tom. "Where does it go?" said Jeff.

_____ Just then Mr. Kay came riding his bike down the path.

_____ The boys parked their bikes and walked down the path.

_____ "Stop by next Sunday and I will get you boys tickets for next week's race," said Mr. Kay. "It'll be one of the best races of the season."

Word Bank

does

down

Do

of

Challenge

Put Word Group 8 in ABC order:

do	oh where does of who
	down old won one

1. _____   2. _____

3. _____   4. _____   5. _____   6. _____

7. _____   8. _____   9. _____   10. _____

Code

Use the animal code to figure out the words below.

a alligator	b bear	c cat	d dog	e elephant	f frog	g goat	h horse	i inchworm
j jaguar	k koala	l ladybug	m monkey	n newt	o octopus	p pig	q quail	r rabbit
s skunk	t tiger	u unicorn	v vulture	w walrus	x xenops	y yak	z zebra	

1. ___ ___ ___ ___

Word Bank

lose	through
because	love
very	book
many	walk
both	money

2. ___ ___ ___ ___

3. ___ ___ ___ ___ ___

4. ___ ___ ___ ___ ___ ___ ___

5. ___ ___ ___ ___

6. ___ ___ ___ ___

Word Group 9 81

Trace/Build/Write

Trace.

walk

Build the word.

Be a Letter Detective. Hunt for the letters that make up the word.
Use newspapers, catalogs, or magazines. Cut the letters
and glue them in order in the space provided.

w	a	l	k

Write the word.

_____

- -

_____

Hidden Picture

What is hidden in the picture?

Follow the Color Code to see what is hidden in the picture.

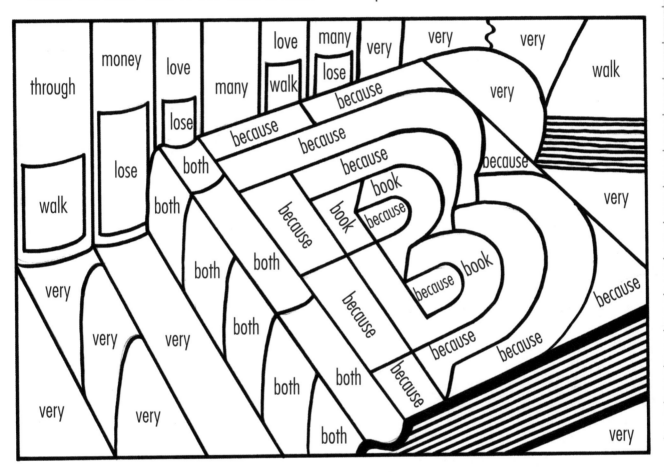

Color Code
because = red
both = green
book = orange
very = brown
walk = dark brown
through = blue
money = light blue
lose = yellow
many = purple
love = pink

Write a sentence about what you find.

_____

_____

_____

_____

Grid

Use the Word Grid to answer the questions.

	A	B	C	D
1	both	many	walk	lose
2	many	walk	lose	both
3	walk	lose	both	many
4	lose	both	many	walk

1. What word is at B4 on the grid?

2. What word is at C2 on the grid?

3. What word is at A3 on the grid?

4. What word is at D1 on the grid?

5. What word is at A4 on the grid?

6. What word is at B1 on the grid?

7. What word is at C3 on the grid?

8. What word is at D2 on the grid?

9. What word is at B4, C3, and D2?

10. What word is at C2, D1, and A4?

Fill in the blank with the correct word.

11. The Jets and the Jazz will play a big game. _____ teams are super!

12. Each team will play hard. No one wants to _____ the game.

Maze

Help Ann find the money she lost. Follow the path where because is the second word and love is the fifth word in the five-word repeated pattern.

Circle the Picture

What can you go through?
Circle each thing you can go through.

Word Search

```
m w n v e r y w l m
o b v t e s g t b h
n w a i b a y h o p
e x l c e o i r t r
y f o k c w m o h z
s e v l a a a u u w
z b e n u l n g y a
f t p m s v y h t l
b o o k e f w j l k
c a r y g l o s e w
```

Use the Word Bank to fill in the blanks.

1. I can go _____ the tunnel.

2. I will _____ home.

3. You need _____ to buy things.

4. It is a _____ pretty day!

Word Bank

lose

through

because

love

very

book

many

walk

both

money

Crossword Puzzle

Word Bank

because	through
money	both
love	book
very	lose
walk	

Across

5. I _____ you!
6. I will read the _____ .
7. You _____ are winners.
8. I will go _____ you asked me.

Down

1. I will go _____ the tunnel.
2. The _____ is in the purse.
3. Gram is _____ old.
4. Will you go for a _____?
5. The team did not _____ .

Story Reading

Saving Money

Ben and Joe are friends. **Both** boys **love** to read **book**s. They like all kinds of **book**s: **book**s about how to draw, **book**s about animals, and **book**s about friends.

One day the phone rang; it was Ben calling. "Hello, Joe, would you like to come to the **book**store with me?" he asked. "They are having a sale," he added.

"Yes," said Joe. "I need a good **book.**"

Ben and Joe went for a **walk** to the **book**store. They looked at all the **book**s. They looked **through** stacks and racks of **book**s. They saw many good **book**s. "I want this **book**," Ben said. "But it costs too much **money**."

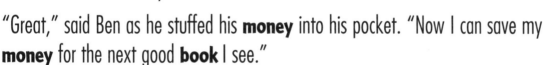

"That is a great **book**," said Joe. "But you don't have to buy it, **because** I have the **very** same one at home. I will let you use it."

"Great," said Ben as he stuffed his **money** into his pocket. "Now I can save my **money** for the next good **book** I see."

"That is good," said Joe. Then he added, "If you don't **lose** it first." Ben looked down at his pocket. His money was sticking out. "Thanks, Joe. You have helped me save my **money** again."

Word Group 9 89

Sequencing and ABC Order

Based on the story you just read, put the sentences in logical order from 1 (the first) to 5 (the last).

_____ They looked through stacks and racks of books.

_____ "I want this book," Ben said. "But it costs too much money."

_____ Ben and Joe went for a walk to the bookstore.

_____ "That is a great book," said Joe. "But you don't have to buy it, because I have the very same one at home. I will let you use it."

_____ Ben and Joe are friends. Both boys love to read books.

Word Bank

very

walk

through

money

love

Put these words in ABC order:

very
walk
through
money
love
book

1. _____   4. _____

2. _____   5. _____

3. _____   6. _____

Challenge

Put Word Group 9 in ABC order:

lose through because love very
book many walk both money

1. _____   6. _____

2. _____   7. _____

3. _____   8. _____

4. _____   9. _____

5. _____   10. _____

90 **Word Group 9**

Code

Use the animal code to figure out the words below.

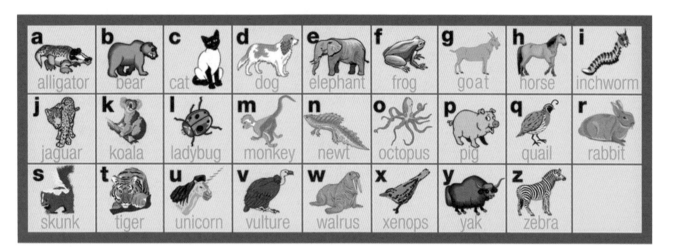

a alligator	b bear	c cat	d dog	e elephant	f frog	g goat	h horse	i inchworm
j jaguar	k koala	l ladybug	m monkey	n newt	o octopus	p pig	q quail	r rabbit
s skunk	t tiger	u unicorn	v vulture	w walrus	x xenops	y yak	z zebra	

1. _____ _____ _____ _____ _____

2. _____ _____ _____

3. _____ _____ _____ _____ _____

4. _____ _____ _____ _____

5. _____ _____ _____

6. _____ _____ _____ _____

Word Bank

climb	new
water	color
now	were
come	some
what	could

Trace/Build/Write

Trace.

were

Build the word.

Be a Letter Detective. Hunt for the letters that make up the word.
Use newspapers, catalogs, or magazines. Cut the letters
and glue them in order in the space provided.

w   e   r   e

Write the word.

Hidden Picture

What is hidden in the picture?

Follow the Color Code to see what is hidden in the picture.

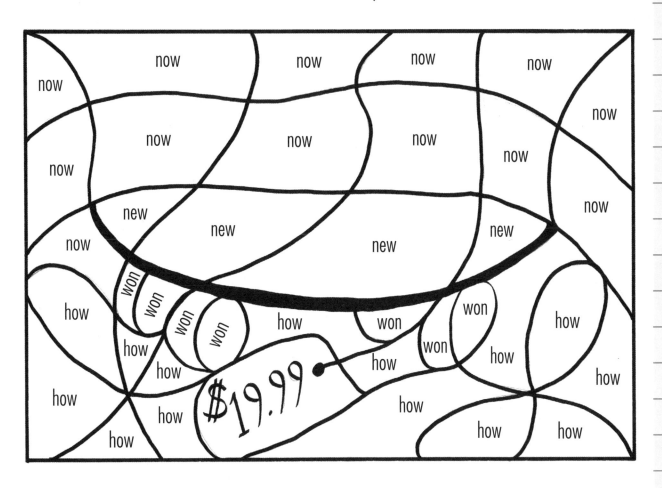

Color Code

new = green

now = blue

how = red

won = brown

Fill in the blank. Look at my new

_____

Grid

Use the Word Grid to answer the questions.

	A	B	C	D
1	climb	come	could	color
2	come	could	color	climb
3	could	color	climb	come
4	color	climb	come	could

1. What word is at B4 on the grid?

2. What word is at D2 on the grid?

3. What word is at A3 on the grid?

4. What word is at C1 on the grid?

5. What word is at D4 on the grid?

6. What word is at B3 on the grid?

7. What word is at C3 on the grid?

8. What word is at A1 on the grid?

9.   Use the word at B4, D2, and C3 and A1 to fill in the blank:

I could _____ the hill.

10.   Use the word at A3, C1 and D4 to fill in the blank:

_____ you?

 Word Group 10

Maze

Help the kids get to the candy store. Follow the path where every third word is **now** and every fifth word is **some** in the five-word repeated pattern.

**You helped the kids get to the store.
Now they can get some candy!**

Circle the Picture

Water, Water, Everywhere!

Circle the things with water.

Word Search

```
g c o l o r k a h l
e r b r v t c w s o
t y c w n s o m e w
w w o e d x p l z n
h c u r n h k c o s
a l l e o i w o d n
t i d c w q a m b e
n m o m l j t e j w
i b b a f s e h z s
w e m p d c r w d l
```

Use the Word Bank to fill in the blanks.

1. May I _____ to the store with you?

2. _____ time is it?

3. Bob can _____ the ladder.

4. It is good to drink _____.

Word Bank

climb	new
water	color
now	were
come	some
what	could

Word Group 10

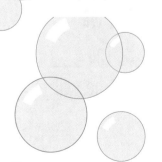

97

Crossword Puzzle

Word Bank

new	color
water	come
now	could
climb	

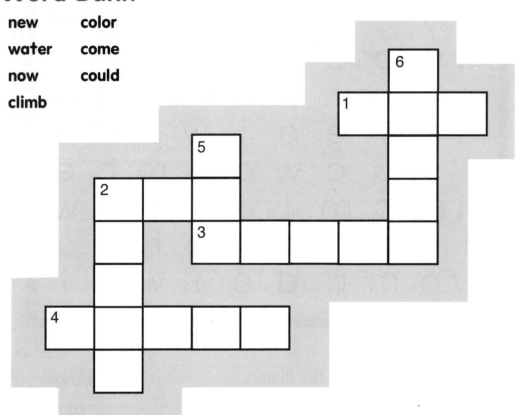

Across

1. It is _____ time to go.
2. I will _____ with you.
3. The _____ tastes good.
4. She will _____ the hill.

Down

2. He _____ not see us hiding.
5. I got a _____ game.
6. Red is a _____.

Story Reading

A New Camping Spot

The Giff family was going on a camping trip to Ross State Park. Mike and Matt Giff **could** not wait to **climb** on the rocks by the stream where the family would set up camp. The Giff family had been to Ross State Park many times, but this year they picked a **new** spot to set up camp. Rocky Stream was a place known to have huge rocks on its bank. When their family got to Rocky Stream, they all **were** excited.

"Look," said Matt. "The rocks are pretty. They have every **color** you can think of in them."

"It is very pretty here," said Mom. "Look how blue the **water** is. It is so pure and clean."

"Let's set up camp," said Dad.

Dad, Mom, and Matt set up camp. They **were** hot and tired. They needed **some** food, too.

"We'll have sandwiches, fruit, and drinks. **What** do you think of that?" asked Mom.

"Yum," said Mike. "I **could** eat about six sandwiches. I am very hungry."

"I **could** eat ten," said Matt.

"Me, too," said Dad.

The family ate. They fished and swam. They had a great time.

For one week they had fun in the great outdoors. On their last day Mike asked, "**Could** we **climb** the hillside and take one last look?"

"Yes," said Dad. "I bet it will be **some**thing up there."

They all **climb**ed the hillside and looked out over the land.

"**What** a pretty place," said Dad. "I am glad we came here to set up camp, and I'm glad we **climb**ed up here."

"Me, too," said Matt. "Can we **come** here again next year?"

Mom and Dad took one last look around. Then, just as if one person were speaking, they said, "Yes, we'll **come** back again next year!"

"Yippee!" cried Matt and Mike. "We **were** hoping you'd say that!"

Sequencing and ABC Order

Based on the story you just read, put the sentences in logical order from 1 (the first) to 5 (the last).

_____ They **were** hot and tired. They needed **some** food, too.

_____ For one week they had fun in the great outdoors. On their last day Mike asked, "**Could** we **climb** the hillside and take one last look?"

_____ The Giff family had been to Ross State Park many times, but this year they picked a **new** spot to set up camp.

_____ When their family got to Rocky Stream, they all **were** excited.

_____ Mom and Dad took one last look around. Then, just as if one person were speaking, they said, "Yes, we'll **come** back again next year!"

Word Bank

new
climb
some
were
come

Put these words in ABC order:

new	climb	some	were

1. _____ 3. _____

2. _____ 4. _____

Challenge

Put Word Group 10 in ABC order:

climb new water color now
were come some what could

1. _____ 6. _____

2. _____ 7. _____

3. _____ 8. _____

4. _____ 9. _____

5. _____ 10. _____

Word Bank

A Walk in the Forest

Word Bank

mother
was
took
through
find
saw
walk

My mom and dad _____ me for a _____ in the forest. We had fun. We saw a deer with white spots. It _____ sleeping, but I stepped on a stick. It went cr-ack! The deer jumped up and ran off _____ the forest. It went to _____ its _____.

1
2
3
4
5
6

Look at the pictures. Order the events from first to last. Write 1, 2, 3, or 4 in the correct space.

Best Friends

Read the story. Use the Word Bank to fill in the blanks.

Word Bank
great
friend
school
my
food
says
by
our

I like _____ friend. My _____
1   2
likes me. We ride the bus to _____
3
each day. We sit side _____ side at
4
lunch. We share our _____. We
5
share _____ jokes. We share our
6
smiles, too. I like my _____. My friend likes me.
7
He _____ that I'm the best. I think that's
8
_____, but I think he is better than the best.
9

Write your answers in ABC order here.

1. _____   2. _____   3. _____

4. _____   5. _____   6. _____

7. _____   8. _____

The Big Old House

There is a big house on my street. It is very old. It makes me feel scared when I see it, because vines climb up the sides and birds use it as their home. Once, I saw a bat go in a broken window, but he didn't stay long. Maybe the poor thing felt scared, just like me, and needed to go home.

Be a Word Detective!

Find these words in the story and circle them.

as	house
old	because
their	very
saw	climb
poor	there

The words form a letter. Write the word from the list that begins with that letter.

Match the Meaning to the Word

1. once more   soon

2. not a long time   again

3. not empty   both

4. this one and that one   full

Use these words to fill in the blanks: full both again soon

1. The mail will come _____.

2. _____ girls are pretty.

3. The glass is _____.

4. I lost my homework,

     so I have to do it _____.

 Mixed Word Group

Fill in the Shaded Boxes

Use the Word Bank to find the best answer.

Word Bank

There	lose	climb	the
away	there	The	to

1. _____ is a tree.

2. _____ is a bird.

3. _____ is a cat.

4. Write the Word Bank word that fits in each box.

_____ cat sees _____ bird up in _____ tree. Up, up, _____ cat will _____ _____ get _____ bird. Go _____, little bird, _____ is no time _____ _____ !

Find the Shoes Hidden in the Picture

Read, and then circle the non-decodable words.

My mom wants me to be dressed up from head to toe. My hair looks great all slicked and spiked, but these shoes, they have got to go.

Word Grid

Use the Word Grid to answer the questions.

	A	B	C	D
1	once	move	every	very
2	move	once	very	every
3	very	every	move	once
4	every	very	once	move

1. What word is at B2 on the grid?

2. What word is at D4 on the grid?

3. What word is at A3 on the grid?

4. What word is at C1 on the grid?

5. What word is at A1 on the grid?

6. What word is at D2 on the grid?

7. What word is at B4 on the grid?

8. What word is at C3 on the grid?

9. Fill in the blank. Use B1 to fill in the blank:

I can _____ the box.

Mixed Word Group 107

Guess What?

Match the sentence to the picture. Circle the picture that best tells about the sentence.

1. "Guess what?" said the frog. "I can hop."

2. "Guess what?" said the kangaroo. "I can hop."

3. "Guess what?" said the rabbit. "I can hop."

4. "Guess what?" said the girl and boy. "We can, too!"

Match the uppercase word with the lowercase word.

5. Guess	what
6. What	guess
7. Too	too

Mixed Word Group

Maze

Help Frog get back home. Hop on the words in the repeated pattern guess, what, too to reach Frog's home.

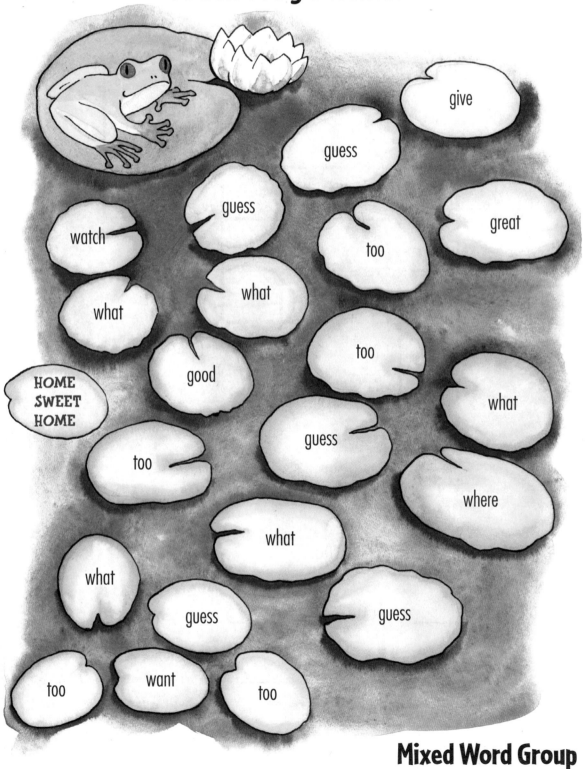

Crossword Puzzle

Word Bank

new	laugh	eye
money	one	lion

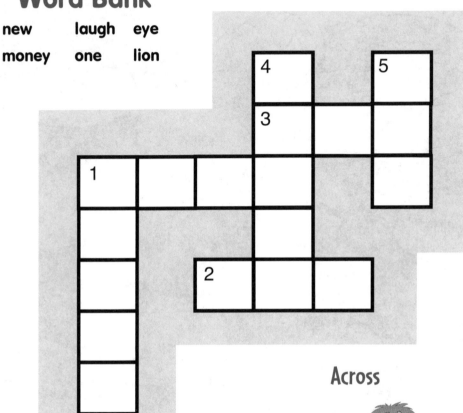

Word Math.
Use 4 down to help you.

2. 4 down = _____ − m o n + e = _____

3. 4 down = _____ − y m = _____

Across

1.   3.

2.

Down

1.   5.

4.

Mixed Word Group

Fill in the Blanks

Shopping

"My _____ and I _____ shopping," said Kim.
₁   ₂

"_____ did you _____?" asked Tam.
₃   ₄

"I got this _____ dress and these _____ that
₅   ₆

_____ on sale."
₇

"Guess what? My dad and I went shopping, too," said

Tam.

"_____ did you _____?" asked Kim.
₈   ₉

"A dress and _____ just like yours," said Tam. "But,
₁₀

shucks, they _____ not on sale."
₁₁

Word Bank

mother
buy
were
What
shoes
pretty

Write the answers in ABC order here.

① _____

② _____

③ _____

④ _____

⑤ _____

⑥ _____

Mixed Word Group 111

Word Grid

Use the Word Grid to answer the questions.

	A	B	C	D
1	of	put	come	now
2	come	now	put	of
3	now	come	of	put
4	put	of	now	come

1. What word is at B4 on the grid?

2. What word is at A2 on the grid?

3. What word is at A1 on the grid?

4. What word is at C4 on the grid?

5. What word is at D2 on the grid?

6. What word is at B1 on the grid?

7. What word is at C3 on the grid?

8. What word is at B4, A1, D2, and C3?

9. Use the answer to number 8 to fill in the blank. Then read the message.

You are one _____ the best at using a grid!

Good job!

Fill in the Blank

Practicing the.
Write The in the blank. Match the picture to the sentence.
Circle the picture that best tells about the sentence.

1. _____hen eats seeds.

2. _____dog sits and begs.

3. _____fish swims.

4. _____cat plays.

5. _____boy runs.

6. _____girl sleeps.

7. Write a sentence for this picture. Use the.

_____

_____

_____

_____

Time to Rhyme

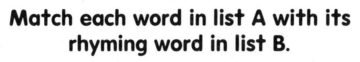

Match each word in list A with its rhyming word in list B.

List A	List B
1. look	how
2. kind	book
3. now	find
4. do	many
5. any	to
6. would	talk
7. oh	know
8. walk	could

**Follow the directions. Fill in the blanks.
Then read the message.**

1. Write the first word in list A.   2. Write the first word in list B.

3. Write the fourth word in list B.   4. Write the seventh word in list B.

1_____   2_____   3_____ rhymes you

4_____ !

Mixed Word Group

Where Is Mother Duck?

"**Look**!" **said** Tom. "A duckling."

"Where is the duckling's **mother**?" asked Max.

"Is she sitting on the nest?" **said** Max.

"No, she is not," **said** Tom.

"Is she eating grain?" asked Max.

"No, she is not," **said** Tom.

"Is she in the barn?" asked Max.

"No, she is not, but I **know** where she is," **said** Tom.

"**Look**!" **said** Tom. "She is swimming in the pond."

Match the picture clues to the word.

know

look

said

mother

Fill in the Shaded Boxes

Use the Word Bank to find the best answer.

Word Bank

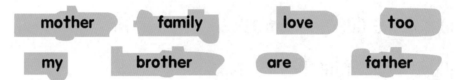

mother   family   love   too

my   brother   are   father

1. My [   ] loves me.

2. My [   ] loves me.

3. My [   ] loves me.

4. I [   ] my mother.

5. I love [   ] father.

6. I love my [   ], too.

7. We [   ] a happy [   ].

8. Write the Word Bank word that fits in this shape box.

   My dog loves me, [   ].

116   **Mixed Word Group**

Word Search

```
m  r  n  b  v  c  l  w  c  d
f  d  c  f  g  o  j  k  l  o
h  o  o  g  w  l  s  o  f  w
d  w  l  d  z  o  x  e  i  p
s  n  i  h  a  r  t  l  n  k
w  y  g  o  o  d  s  b  d  r
h  i  m  a  l  l  p  o  a  e
o  w  s  h  a  v  e  w  d  p
s  o  m  e  l  b  o  g  i  b
t  v  r  o  y  o  u  r  f  m
```

Word Bank

you	who
good	color
have	all
down	some
your	find

Use the Word Bank to fill in the blanks.

Did _____ _____ them _____?

Words to Know

Help the Dog Get Home

Word Bank
answer
circle
find
story
write
around

Directions:
1. Walk down the path.
2. Go past a tree and around the fountain.
3. Find a bone by a tree.
4. Go past the fence with the cat sitting on it.
5. Walk in a circle around the pond. You are home.

1. What is the dog's name?
   Follow the directions to find out.
2. Write the letter that is on the bone. _____
3. Write the letter that is on the fence. _____
4. Write the letter that is on the tree. _____
5. Write the letter that is on the pond. _____
6. What name do the letters spell? Write it here in the blank. _____

Write a story about the dog.

_____

_____

_____

_____

Be a
Word Detective!

Find and circle these words in the poem below.

At the Zoo

It is great to go to the zoo.
There is always a lot to see.
It's fun to watch each animal
do what they do best:
run, leap, climb, sleep,
or kerplash!

Word Bank	
there	watch
animal	do
what	climb
zoo	always
they	great
to	

Fill in the blanks.

Use the word that was used **twice** that fills in the blank. Read the sentence.

What _____ you _____ best?

Draw a
picture
to answer
the
question.

Only One Out

The batter steps **to the** plate. Crack, **the** bat hits **the** ball. **Through the** air it sails. I raise **my** mitt, and plop, into **my** hand it goes. **The** batter is **out**. **Only one out was** needed. **Now** we **have won the** game!

Write the answer:

1. What sport was being played?

_____

_____

2. What are the clues that help you know?

_____

_____

_____

_____

3. How many outs did the losing team have at the start of the story?

_____

_____

Homonym Match

Homonyms are words that sound the same but have different meanings.

won — to get the prize   one — the first

by — near, beside   buy — get by paying a price

there — in that place   their — belonging to them

to — in the direction of   too — also

Circle the word with the correct meaning to fill in the blank.

1. I (by, buy) **gum at the store.**

2. (Their, There) **houses are down the street.**

3. **The best team** (one, won) **the game.**

4. **My dog is white and black,** (too, to).

5. **He sits** (by, buy) **the teacher.**

6. **She can go** (their, there) **with you.**

7. (One, Won) **dog is sleeping.**

8. **She goes** (too, to) **see her friend.**

Mixed Word Group 121

Circle the Picture

Which one is pretty?
Circle the correct answer.

1

a b

2
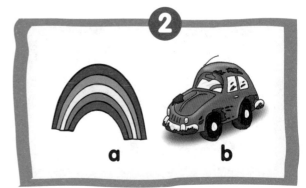
a b

3

a b

4

a b

5

a b

6
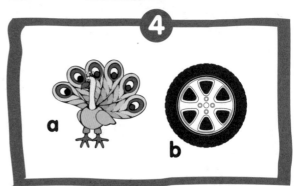
a b

7

a b

8

a b

Mixed Word Group

Fill in the Shaded Boxes

Fill in the answer to the riddle.

1. They help you. They play with you.
   Who are they?

   A _____

2. It goes up. It goes down. It can be big
   or small. What is it?

   A _____

3. They keep your feet from getting wet. They keep your feet from
   getting hurt. What are they?

4. It is a place where you can see animals. It is a place that keeps
   animals safe. What is it?

   A _____

5. It has pages. It can be long or short. What is it?

   A _____

Mixed Word Group 123

Word Family Fun

Use these letters to make new words.
Add t, m, sh, c, gr, sm, w, b, r, f, n, cr, br, h,
or bl to the word family.

1.

all
ball
all
_____
_____
_____
_____
_____

2.

ook
look
book
took
_____
_____
_____
_____
_____

3.

ould
would
could
_____
_____
_____
_____
_____

4.

ind
kind
find
_____
_____
_____
_____
_____

Mixed Word Group

The Lost Ball

"I lost my ball," said Max. "Kim, would you help me find it?" he asked.

"Yes," said Kim. "I will help you find it. Did you look in the yard?" she asked.

"Yes, I did look in the yard, but not under the bush," said Max.

"Here it is. I kicked it into the bush last week and I forgot all about it. Thanks for helping me find my ball. You are the best at helping friends find what they lost," said Max.

"Thanks, but I didn't do much to help," said Kim.

"I could not find my ball, and now I have it. You were a big help," said Max with a smile.

1. What did Max lose?

2. Where was it?

3. Who helped him find it?

What Luck

Dan woke up and jumped **out of** bed. This **was the** day he had waited for **all** week. Dan started **to** get dressed, but **where was** Dan's blue shirt?

"Mom, **where** is **my** blue team shirt?" asked Dan. "**The one** with **the lion** on it."

"**Look** on **the** rack," said Mom. "Is it hanging **there**?"

Dan **look**ed on **the** rack. "No," **said** Dan. "It is not hanging on **the** rack."

"**Look** in **the** stack," **said** Mom. Dan **look**ed in the stack. No blue shirt.

"**Oh**, no!" **said** Dan. "I will not get **my picture** taken with **the** team."

"Well," **said** Mom. "**There** is no time **to look**. It is late. **The** bus will be here **soon**. **Put** on a shirt. **Find any** blue **one** and **put** it on, so **you** will not be late."

Dan dashed **around the house**. He ate, and brushed his teeth. He had **done almost all** he needed **to do**. Dan needed **only to find** a blue shirt. He reached in a pile **of** clothes he had not **put** in his dresser. He grabbed for **some**thing blue. **To** his surprise, **there** it **was**, his blue team shirt with **the lion** on it!

"Mom! Mom!" he yelled. "**Look**! It's **my** team shirt!"

Mom smiled. "That's **great**!" she **said**.

"What luck!" **said** Dan, with an ear-to-ear smile.

Mixed Word Group

Sequencing and ABC Order

Based on the story you just read, put the sentences in logical order from 1 (the first) to 5 (the last).

_____ Dan started to get dressed, but where was Dan's blue shirt?

_____ "Find any blue one and put it on, so you will not be late."

_____ Dan woke up and jumped out of bed.

_____ "Mom! Mom!" he yelled. "Look!! It's my team shirt!"

_____ "Look on the rack," said Mom. "Is it hanging there?"

Word Bank

put

where

out

Look

there

Put these words in ABC order:

1. _____ 2. _____ 3. _____

4. _____ 5. _____

put

where

out

look

there

Word Group 1

Answer Key

Page 1 — Code

    1. full 2. out 3. picture 4. zoo 5. your
    6. father

Page 2 — Trace/Build/Write

    give

Page 3 — Hidden Picture

    butterfly

Page 4 — Grid

    1. out 2. poor 3. picture 4. picture
    5. picture 6. poor 7. out 8. friend
    9. picture 10. poor 11. out

Page 5 — Maze

    friend

Page 6 — Circle the Picture

    1. A full glass. 2. A full bowl. 3. A full cup.
    4. A bag heaped to the top. 5. An egg carton
    with a full dozen. 6. A full jar. 7. A full box of
    crayons. 8. A full container of juice.

Page 7 — Word Search

a	f	e	t	p	m	f	u	l	l
z	a	k	l	r	q	m	p	y	o
o	t	n	f	e	p	a	l	c	b
o	h	o	g	t	g	o	f	b	y
r	e	u	w	t	d	v	r	d	o
p	r	t	n	y	l	c	i	s	u
y	o	u	s	i	l	f	e	p	r
p	o	o	r	x	t	r	n	l	t
h	f	z	g	i	v	e	d	u	e
u	p	i	c	t	u	r	e	f	p

    1. friend 2. pretty 3. give 4. poor

Page 8 — Crossword Puzzle

Across
3. father
7. picture
8. your
9. zoo

Down
1. give
2. full
3. friend

4. out
5. poor
6. pretty

Page 10 — Sequencing and ABC Order

4 "Here, Dad, I made this pretty picture just for you."
2 Jess got out her sketchpad.
1 Jess went to the zoo with her father.
5 I am going to keep the rest to help me think of my trip to the zoo.
3 She made a picture for Gram.

Words in ABC order:

1. father
2. give

3. out
4. poor

5. your
6. zoo

Challenge: Word Group 1 in ABC order

father	friend	full	give	out	picture	poor	pretty	your	zoo
1	2	3	4	5	6	7	8	9	10

Word Group 1 129

Word Group 2

Answer Key

Page 11 — Code

    1. only 2. would 3. around 4. every
    5. you 6. draw

Page 12 — Trace/Build/Write

    once

Page 13 — Hidden Picture

    pencil and paper on a table

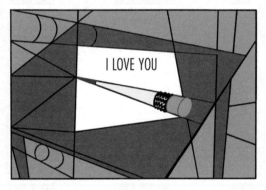

Page 14 — Grid

    1. you 2. our 3. our 4. our 5. every
    6. family 7. you 8. you 9. You

Page 15 — Maze

    family

Page 16 — Circle the Picture

    1. fan 2. swivel chair 3. carousel 4. Ferris
wheel 5. windmill 6. game spinner 7. train
on a circular track

Page 17 — Word Search

a	d	k	w	f	e	r	y	o	u
r	f	w	o	e	b	o	d	e	g
o	l	y	u	v	s	u	y	d	r
u	t	d	l	e	i	r	x	r	t
n	p	u	d	r	r	p	p	a	q
d	j	h	i	y	t	o	o	w	u
t	e	o	n	c	e	v	n	p	i
n	o	u	f	a	m	i	l	y	m
s	m	s	w	e	d	f	y	n	b
v	c	w	r	i	t	e	o	r	c

1. write 2. around 3. only 4. draw

Page 18 — Crossword Puzzle

Across		Down	
1. our	4. would	1. only	8. once
2. family	5. every	6. draw	9. write
3. you		7. around	

Page 20 — Sequencing and ABC Order

5 Dad smiled. "It's a joke," he said. "I do not like to ride rides that spin. But it was fun getting the two of you going around and around."

2 "I would like to ride things that do not go around," said Ron. "Me, too," said Mom.

1 "Ron, would you like to go to Kidsland Park for our summer trip?" asked Mom.

3 "Just ride it once with me, Ron. Please?" said Dad.

4 "Once I draw your name, you have to ride it."

Words in ABC order:

1. around	3. every	5. write
2. draw	4. family	6. you

Challenge: Word Group 2 in ABC order

around	draw	every	family	once	only	our	write	would	you
1	2	3	4	5	6	7	8	9	10

Word Group 2 131

Word Group 3

Answer Key

Page 21 — Code

    1. story 2. house 3. guess 4. animal
    5. talk 6. always

Page 22 — Trace/Build/Write

    The; any reasonable response

Page 23 — Hidden Picture

    House; any reasonable response

Page 24 — Grid

    1. all 2. all 3. have 4. the 5. talk 6. all
    7. the 8. all 9. all 10. the 11. Have

Page 25 — Maze

    Path marked with pattern
    again, all, have, talk.

Page 26 — Circle the Picture

    monkey, bird, porcupine, lion, elephant, fish,
    iguana, giraffe, ostrich, and turtle

Page 27 — Word Search

g	m	e	d	s	z	s	o	a	y
u	a	t	a	l	k	t	n	l	c
e	g	h	b	q	s	o	l	w	k
s	a	e	f	v	c	r	j	a	g
s	i	h	q	w	l	y	e	y	a
o	n	y	u	e	h	o	u	s	e
t	a	n	i	m	a	l	i	v	a
y	m	t	h	a	v	f	t	a	l
e	r	e	d	n	e	s	d	m	l
a	n	x	c	v	k	p	i	r	w

1. animal 2. house 3. guess 4. always

Page 28 — Crossword Puzzle

Across

3. again   7. talk

5. animal   8. guess

6. house

Down

1. story   3. always

2. have   4. all

Page 30 — Sequencing and ABC Order

4 "All that work has made me hot and tired, I have to sit," said Mrs. Tweed.

3 The sun rose high in the sky.

5 "I'm glad we stopped to hear them tell us a brand new story and sing their pretty tune."

1 "I guess we better get to work," said Mr. Tweed.

2 "The house always looks pretty when the grass is cut and the weeds are pulled,"
said Mrs. Tweed.

Words in ABC order:

1. all   2. guess   3. house   4. story   5. the

Challenge: Word Group 3 in ABC order

again	all	always	animal	guess	have	house	story	talk	the
1	2	3	4	5	6	7	8	9	10

Word Group 3 133

Word Group 4

Answer Key

Page 31 — Code

     1. know 2. how 3. answer 4. about
     5. there 6. any

Page 32 — Trace/Build/Write

     they

Page 33 — Hidden Picture

Sunglasses and 3 boats out in the water

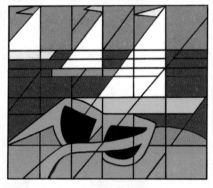

Page 34 — Grid

     1. they 2. know 3. are 4. how 5. know
     6. they 7. how 8. are 9. know 10. are

Page 35 — Maze

     1. there 2.Their 3. their 4. there 5. there
     6. their 7. their 8. there 9. their 10. there

Page 36 — Circle the Picture

     1. sharing 2. child helping to clean up 3. giving flower 4. child smiling 5. helping to carry
     6. easing door 7. hugging 8. all playing

Page 37 — Word Search

t	h	e	r	e	a	b	o	u	t
s	n	b	i	d	s	h	d	k	a
a	q	a	r	s	t	o	t	n	r
n	r	w	k	a	h	w	u	o	e
y	p	t	i	u	e	v	l	w	o
j	l	g	n	y	i	f	e	j	n
h	o	e	d	m	r	g	y	i	y
r	p	q	s	g	h	x	e	o	r
w	t	h	e	y	w	q	r	z	t
e	n	f	l	a	n	s	w	e	r
m	h	i	o	c	e	l	d	k	s

     1. answer 2. they 3. know

Page 38 — Crossword Puzzle

Across

1. know   5. any

2. answer   7. there

4. they

Down

1. kind   4. their

2. about   5. are

3. How   6. eye

Page 40 — Sequencing and ABC Order

4   The next day in art class their teacher, Mr. Hartnett, had them make portrait paintings.

2   "They seem to be keeping their eye on us."

5   The students in their class liked how they made their paintings give them the eye.

1   "Look, there are all kinds of people on the wall in here," said Quinn.

3   "Yes, let's get the clerk," said Jake. "I need to know more about these strange paintings."

Words in ABC order:

1. answer   4. kind

2. eye   5. they

3. how

Challenge: Word Group 4 in ABC order

about	answer	any	are	eye	how	kind	know
1	2	3	4	5	6	7	8

their	there	they
9	10	11

Word Group 4   135

Word Group 5

Answer Key

Page 41 — Code

    1. saw   2. good   3. shoes   4. find   5. says
    6. put

Page 42 — Trace/Build/Write

    said; Go to bed; child's name

Page 43 — Hidden Picture

    school

Page 44 — Grid

    1. put   2. great   3. put   4. put   5. saw
    6. says   7. says   8. saw   9. Put   10. saw
    11. great

Page 45 — Maze

    great, good repeated
    either great or good
    either great or good

Page 46 — Circle the Picture

    1. tennis shoes   2. tap shoes   3. hiking boots
    4. sandals   5. dress shoes   6. spikes
    7. flippers   8. work boots

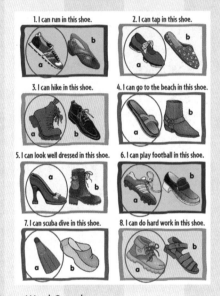

Page 47 — Word Search

    1. saw   2. soon   3. said   4. Put

Page 48 — Crossword Puzzle

Across
1. school
3. great
5. soon

Down
1. shoes
2. find
3. good
4. said

Page 50 — Sequencing and ABC Order

5 "I can go!" said Cam. "I can't wait to get to Vick's."

1 Cam saw Jen ride her bike up to the house.

3 "Just last week my mother said I need a little bit of everything: shoes, pants, shirts, and underclothes."

4 "I'll go in and ask if I can go with you. I will be out soon," said Cam.

2 "Look, Cam!" said Jen. "The ad says, 'Don't miss Vick's Back to School Sale.'"

Words in ABC order:
1. find
2. great
3. put
4. says

Challenge: Word Group 5 in ABC order

find	good	great	put	said	saw	says	school	shoes	soon
1	2	3	4	5	6	7	8	9	10

Word Group 5 137

Word Group 6

Answer Key

Page 51 — Code

    1. move   2. buy   3. mother   4. want
    5. circle   6. brother

Page 52 — Trace/Build/Write

    was

Page 53 — Hidden Picture

    A circle.

Page 54 — Grid

    1. by   2. my   3. by   4. buy   5. watch
    6. my   7. my   8. by   9. by   10. my

Page 55 — Maze

    by

Page 56 — Circle the Picture

    1. bike   2. cat   3. striped dress   4. ice cream
    5. fish   6. bird

Any reasonable response

1. The thing I want has wheels.
2. The thing I want has fur.
3. The thing I want is striped.
4. The thing I want is sweet.
5. The thing I want has gills.
6. The thing I want has a beak.

Page 57 — Word Search

```
w  a  s  t  r  l  v  n  w  z
o  k  b  c  m  v  b  m  a  k
m  o  v  e  o  i  y  c  n  x
b  e  c  s  t  b  w  m  k  o
u  w  i  l  h  t  b  y  t  w
z  q  r  f  e  a  u  i  g  a
a  y  c  t  r  d  y  s  f  t
w  d  l  w  a  n  t  i  d  c
b  h  e  d  f  h  o  p  n  h
r  b  r  o  t  h  e  r  e  y
```

1. circle 2. mother 3. watch 4. buy

Page 58 — Crossword Puzzle

Across	Down
1. was	1. want
2. watch	3. my
3. mother	4. buy
4. brother	5. move
5. by	6. circle

Page 60 — Sequencing and ABC Order

3   Each time he went shopping, Mr. Zimmer stopped by The Game Zone.

1   Devin Zimmer, his mother, and his brother Smith all liked to play games.

4   He liked to watch them move around the game board, each trying to reach the winner's circle first.

5   When people asked if he liked games, Mr. Zimmer would say, "My family likes games. I just like to watch them have fun."

2   Mr. Zimmer did not like to play games, but he liked to buy games for his family.

Words in ABC order:

1. by	3. my
2. circle	4. was

Challenge: Word Group 6 in ABC order

brother	buy	by	circle	mother	move	my	want	was	watch
1	2	3	4	5	6	7	8	9	10

Word Group 6   139

Word Group 7

Answer Key

Page 61 — Code

    1. to 2. look 3. as 4. took 5. away 6. too

Page 62 — Trace/Build/Write

    laugh

Page 63 — Hidden Picture

    lion

Page 64 — Grid

    1. too 2. ball 3. as 4. ball 5. to 6. to
    7. to 8. too 9. to, ball, too

Page 65 — Maze

    away, food, took, ball, as written in a repeated pattern

Page 66 — Circle the Picture

    All the foods; any reasonable response

Page 67 — Word Search

a	y	s	t	o	o	p	e	v	b
t	m	l	d	n	c	j	f	c	a
a	n	a	l	i	o	n	o	x	l
w	b	u	i	b	s	r	p	o	r
a	g	g	t	g	w	i	b	l	r
y	l	h	k	h	z	t	n	o	c
w	i	e	q	r	k	o	m	o	t
t	b	a	l	l	f	o	y	k	o
v	a	s	p	h	y	k	d	y	u
f	o	o	d	x	l	t	g	b	k

    1. lion 2. food 3. took 4. away

Page 68 — Crossword Puzzle

Across	Down
2. laugh	1. food
3. took	2. look

Page 70 — Sequencing and ABC Order

3 "I hear you would like to have a friend," said the little bird.

1 Lion wished for a friend to play with.

4 "Can you teach me how to do all those neat things with a ball?" asked Lion.

2 As soon as he said his wish, a little bird perched in a tree.

5 They each went away smiling, knowing that they had made a friend.

Words in ABC order:

1. as	4. laugh
2. ball	5. took
3. food	

Challenge: Word Group 7 in ABC order

as	away	ball	food	laugh	lion	look	to	too	took
1	2	3	4	5	6	7	8	9	10

Word Group 7 141

Word Group 8

Answer Key

Page 71 — Code

    1. of 2. down 3. oh 4. old 5. does
    6. where

Page 72 — Trace/Build/Write

    who

Page 73 — Hidden Picture

    one and two

Page 74 — Grid

    1. of 2. of 3. of 4. of 5. oh 6. oh
    7. do 8. does 9. of

Page 75 — Maze

    does

Page 76 — Circle the Picture

    1. ride a bike 2. tie shoes 3. swim
    4. read a book 5. sleep 6. catch a ball
    7. skate 8. hop

Page 77 — Word Search

```
p  w  i  g  v  o  h  b  d  o
g  h  o  h  d  o  k  g  d  v
u  o  p  j  o  s  f  s  w  e
g  r  a  k  e  a  i  w  l  s
o  n  e  l  s  h  o  t  i  x
q  t  s  z  b  q  l  r  f  j
w  y  d  x  n  n  d  s  d  o
d  o  w  n  m  m  y  w  t  o
e  u  f  r  k  c  o  o  p  f
w  h  e  r  e  d  v  n  c  l
```

1. down 2. Who 3. one

Page 78 — Crossword Puzzle

Across	Down
2. won	1. do
5. old	2. who
6. where	3. down
7. one	4. does

Page 80 — Sequencing and ABC Order

3 "I know that shed," said Tom. "It belongs to Mr. Kay." "Do you know him?" asked Jeff.

1 "Look! A path," said Tom. "Where does it go?" said Jeff.

4 Just then Mr. Kay came riding his bike down the path.

2 The boys parked their bikes and walked down the path.

5 "Stop by next Sunday and I will get you boys tickets for next week's race," said Mr. Kay. "It'll be one of the best races of the season."

Challenge: Word Group 8 in ABC order

do	does	down	of	oh	old	one	where	who	won
1	2	3	4	5	6	7	8	9	10

Word Group 9

Answer Key

Page 81 — Code

    1. many 2. very 3. money 4. through
    5. lose 6. both

Page 82 — Trace/Build/Write

    walk

Page 83 — Hidden Picture

    book/books

    Any sentence about a book

Page 84 — Grid

    1. both 2. lose 3. walk 4. lose 5. lose
    6. many 7. both 8. both 9. both 10. lose
    11. Both 12. lose

Page 85 — Maze

    many, because, very, money, love written in a
    repeated pattern

Page 86 — Circle the Picture

    1. tunnel 2. gate 3. toll booth 4. doorway
    5. turnstile 6. archway 7. airport security
    scanner 8. drawbridge

Page 87 — Word Search

m	w	n	v	e	r	y	w	l	m
o	b	v	t	e	s	g	t	b	h
n	w	a	i	b	a	y	h	o	p
e	x	l	c	e	o	i	r	t	r
y	f	o	k	c	w	m	o	h	z
s	e	v	l	a	a	a	u	u	w
z	b	e	n	u	l	n	g	y	a
f	t	p	m	s	v	y	h	t	l
b	o	o	k	e	f	w	j	l	k
c	a	r	y	g	l	o	s	e	w

    1. through 2. walk 3. money 4. very

Page 88 — Crossword Puzzle

Across
5. love
6. book
7. both
8. because

Down
1. through
2. money
3. very
4. walk
5. lose

Page 89 — Sequencing and ABC Order

3 They looked through stacks and racks of books.
4 "I want this book," Ben said. "But it costs too much money."
2 Ben and Joe went for a walk to the bookstore.
5 "That is a great book," said Joe. "But you don't have to buy it, because
   I have the very same one at home. I will let you use it."
1 Ben and Joe are friends. Both boys love to read books.

Words in ABC order:

1. book
2. love
3. money

4. through
5. very
6. walk

Challenge: Word Group 9 in ABC order

because	book	both	lose	love	many	money	through	very	walk
1	2	3	4	5	6	7	8	9	10

Word Group 9 145

Word Group 10

Answer Key

Page 91 — Code

    1. color 2. new 3. could 4. what 5. now

    6. come

Page 92 — Trace/Build/Write

    were

Page 93 — Hidden Picture

    A new skateboard with a price tag on it

    skateboard

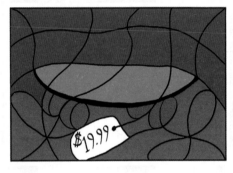

Page 94 — Grid

    1. climb 2. climb 3. could 4. could 5. could

    6. color 7. climb 8. climb 9. climb 10. could

Page 95 — Maze

    color, come, now, were, some in a repeated pattern

Page 96 — Circle the Picture

Page 97 — Word Search

g	c	o	l	o	r	k	a	h		l
e	r	b	r	v	t	c	w	s		o
t	y	c	w	n	s	o	m	e		w
w	w	o	e	d	x	p	l	z		n
h	c	u	r	n	h	k	c	o		s
a	l	l	e	o	i	w	o	d		n
t	i	d	c	w	q	a	m	b		e
n	m	o	m	l	j	t	e	j		w
i	b	b	a	f	s	e	h	z		s
w	e	m	p	d	c	r	w	d		l

1. come 2. What 3. climb 4. water

Page 98 — Crossword Puzzle

Across
1. now
2. come
3. water
4. climb

Down
2. could
3. new
4. color

Page 100 — Sequencing and ABC Order

3 They were hot and tired. They needed some food, too.

4 For one week they had fun in the great outdoors. On their last day Mike asked, "Could we climb the hillside and take one last look?"

1 The Giff family had been to Ross State Park many times, but this year they picked a new spot to set up camp.

2 When their family got to Rocky Stream, they all were excited.

5 Mom and Dad took one last look around. Then, just as if one person were speaking, they said, "Yes, we'll come back again next year!"

Words in ABC order:

1. climb
2. new

3. some
4. were

Challenge: Word Group 10 in ABC order

climb	color	come	could	new	now	some	water	were	what
1	2	3	4	5	6	7	8	9	10

Mixed Word Group

Answer Key

Page 101 — A Walk in the Forest

1. took 2. walk 3. was 4. through 5. find
6. mother

 3

 1

 4

 2

Page 102 — Best Friends

1. my 2. friend 3. school 4. by 5. food
6. our 7. friend 8. says 9. great

Words in ABC order:

1. by 2. food 3. friend 4. great 5. my
6. our 7. says 8. school

Page 103 — The Big Old House

Word Detective words: There, house, very, old, because, climb, as, their, saw, poor

very

Page 104 — Match the Meaning to the Word

1. again 2. soon 3. full 4. both

1. soon 2. Both 3. full 4. again

Page 105 — Fill in the Shaded Boxes

1–3 There

The cat sees the bird up in the tree.

Up, up, the cat will climb to get the bird.

Go away, little bird. There is no time to lose!

Page 106 — Find the Shoes in the Hidden Picture

Non-decodable words:
wants   head   My
My   looks   to
all   shoes   great
have   to   they

Page 107 — Word Grid

1. once 2. move 3. very 4. every 5. once
6. every 7. very 8. move 9. move

Page 108 — Guess What?

1. frog 2. kangaroo 3. rabbit 4. girl and boy
5. Guess-guess 6. What-what 7. Too-too

Page 109 — Maze

guess, what, too in a repeated pattern

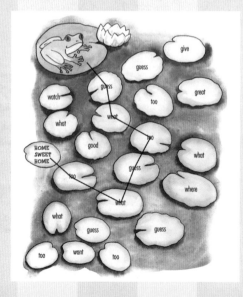

Mixed Word Group 149

Mixed Word Group
Answer Key

Page 115 — Where Is Mother Duck?

Matching: 1. know—head/brain   2. look—eye
3. said—mouth   4. mother—woman shopping

Page 116 — Fill in the Shaded Boxes

1. mother   2. father   3. brother   4. love
5. my   6. brother   7. are, family   8. too

Page 117 — Word Search

m	r	n	b	v	c	l	w	c	d
f	d	c	f	g	o	j	k	l	o
h	o	o	g	w	l	s	o	f	w
d	w	l	d	z	o	x	e	i	p
s	n	i	h	a	r	t	l	n	k
w	y	g	o	o	d	s	b	d	r
h	i	m	a	l	l	p	o	a	e
o	w	s	h	a	v	e	w	d	p
s	o	m	e	l	b	o	g	i	b
t	v	r	o	y	o	u	r	f	m

Did you find them all?

Page 118 — Words to Know

2. s   3. p   4. o   5. t   6. spot

Page 119 — Word Detective

At the Zoo

It is great to go to the zoo. There is always a lot
to see. It's fun to watch each animal do what they
do best: run, leap, climb, sleep, or kerplash!

do

Page 120 — Only One Out

1. baseball 2. mitt, bat, plate, batter, hits
3. two

Page 121 — Homonym Match

1. buy 2. Their 3. won 4. too 5. by
6. there 7. One 8. to

Page 122 — Circle the Picture

1. flower 2. rainbow 3. ring 4. peacock
5. fairy princess 6. crystal 7. fancy card
8. shiny heart

Page 123 — Fill in the Blank

1. friend 2. ball 3. shoes 4. zoo 5. book

Page 124 — Word Family Fun

1. all: ball/all; tall, mall, call, small, wall, fall, hall

2. ook: look/book/took; shook, cook, nook, crook, brook, hook

3. ould: would/could; should

4. ind: kind/find; mind, grind, bind, rind, hind, blind

Page 125 — The Lost Ball

1. Max lost his ball. 2. It was under the bush.
3. Kim helped him find it.

Page 127 — Shaded Boxes, Sequencing, and ABC Order

2 Dan started to get dressed, but where was Dan's blue shirt?

4 "Find any blue one and put it on, so you will not be late."

1 Dan woke up and jumped out of bed.

5 "Mom! Mom!" he yelled. "Look! It's my team shirt!"

3 "Look on the rack," said Mom. "Is it hanging there?"

Words in ABC order:

1. look   4. there
2. out   5. where
3. put

Mixed Word Group 151

Give Your Children a Smart Start...

Making the Grade

Only $14.95 each

Everything Your Elementary Grader Needs to Know

What are the most important concepts and skills your child should know in each grade? How can you teach these fundamentals and make the lessons fun and interesting? **Making the Grade** are groundbreaking new curriculum guides offering a unique approach grounded in everyday life.

Written by authorities in elementary education and state learning standards, each book offers a solid foundation in the fundamentals of a good education in four key areas: **Promoting Literacy** (reading, writing, listening, and speaking), **Science**, **Math**, and **Social Studies**.

Every volume contains clear, step-by-step lessons, dozens of games, puzzles, and hands-on and Internet activities. Tests and answers, checklist reviews, and hundreds of full-color illustrations and charts are also included in each volume. Advice on how to best explain concepts, perforated pages so the books can be shared, and recommended readings round out these practical, appealing guides.

Each book: Paperback, approx. 380 pp., $14.95, Canada $21.95

Everything Your Kindergartner Needs to Know
Daniel A. Van Beek, ISBN 0-7641-2475-7

Everything Your 1st Grader Needs to Know
Laura B. Tyle, ISBN 0-7641-2476-5

Everything Your 2nd Grader Needs to Know
Elena R. Arrigo, ISBN 0-7641-2477-3

Everything Your 3rd Grader Needs to Know
Micki Pflug, ISBN 0-7641-2478-1

Everything Your 4th Grader Needs to Know
Robert R. Roth, ISBN 0-7641-2480-3

Everything Your 5th Grader Needs to Know
Katherine Ermitage, ISBN 0-7641-2481-1

Everything Your 6th Grader Needs to Know
Carol Karton, ISBN 0-7641-2483-8

All prices are in U.S. and Canadian dollars and subject to change without notice. Books may be purchased at your bookseller, or order direct adding 18% postage (minimum charge $5.95). New York, New Jersey, Michigan, Tennessee, and California residents add sales tax.

To order toll-free: 1-800-645-3476 or visit our web site at www.barronseduc.com

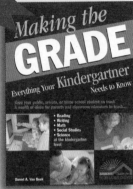
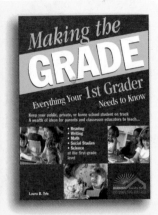

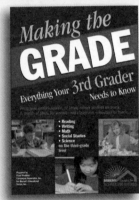
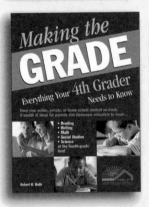
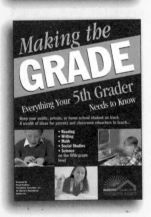

Barron's Educational Series, Inc.
250 Wireless Blvd.,
Hauppauge, NY 11788
Order by Fax: 631-434-8067

In Canada:
Georgetown Book Warehouse
34 Armstrong Ave.
Georgetown, Ontario L7G 4R9
Order toll-free:
1-800-247-7160